W0036131

SAGE was founded in 1965 by Sara Miller McCune to support the dissemination of usable knowledge by publishing innovative and high-quality research and teaching content. Today, we publish over 900 journals, including those of more than 400 learned societies, more than 800 new books per year, and a growing range of library products including archives, data, case studies, reports, and video. SAGE remains majority-owned by our founder, and after Sara's lifetime will become owned by a charitable trust that secures our continued independence.

Los Angeles | London | New Delhi | Singapore | Washington DC | Melbourne

LOCAL FINANCE, FISCAL DECENTRALISATION AND DECENTRALISED PLANNING

Thank you for choosing a SAGE product!
If you have any comment, observation or feedback,
I would like to personally hear from you.

Please write to me at **contactceo@sagepub.in**

Vivek Mehra, Managing Director and CEO, SAGE India.

Bulk Sales

SAGE India offers special discounts
for purchase of books in bulk.
We also make available special imprints
and excerpts from our books on demand.

For orders and enquiries, write to us at

Marketing Department
SAGE Publications India Pvt Ltd
B1/I-1, Mohan Cooperative Industrial Area
Mathura Road, Post Bag 7
New Delhi 110044, India

E-mail us at **marketing@sagepub.in**

Subscribe to our mailing list
Write to **marketing@sagepub.in**

This book is also available as an e-book.

LOCAL FINANCE, FISCAL DECENTRALISATION AND DECENTRALISED PLANNING

A Kerala Experience

B. A. PRAKASH

Los Angeles | London | New Delhi
Singapore | Washington DC | Melbourne

Copyright © B. A. Prakash, 2020

All rights reserved. No part of this book may be reproduced or utilized in any form or by any means, electronic or mechanical, including photocopying, recording or by any information storage or retrieval system, without permission in writing from the publisher.

First published in 2020 by

SAGE Publications India Pvt Ltd
B1/I-1 Mohan Cooperative Industrial Area
Mathura Road, New Delhi 110 044, India
www.sagepub.in

SAGE Publications Inc
2455 Teller Road
Thousand Oaks, California 91320, USA

SAGE Publications Ltd
1 Oliver's Yard, 55 City Road
London EC1Y 1SP, United Kingdom

SAGE Publications Asia-Pacific Pte Ltd
18 Cross Street #10-10/11/12
China Square Central
Singapore 048423

Published by Vivek Mehra for SAGE Publications India Pvt Ltd. Typeset in 10.5/13 pt Berkeley by Zaza Eunice, Hosur, Tamil Nadu, India.

Library of Congress Control Number: 2020930413

ISBN: 978-93-5388-306-5 (HB)

SAGE Team: Rajesh Dey, Syed Husain Naqvi, Madhurima Thapa

CONTENTS

LIST OF ILLUSTRATIONS

FIGURES

TABLES

LIST OF ABBREVIATIONS

AMC	Annual maintenance contract
APL	Above poverty line
BP	Block panchayat
BPL	Below poverty line
BSUP	Basic Services to Urban Poor
BT	Black topped
CSS	Centrally sponsored schemes
D&O	Dangerous and offensive
DP	District panchayat
DPC	District planning committees
DTEs	Developing and transition economies
GDP	Gross domestic product
GF	Gap fund
GoK	Government of Kerala
GP	Gram panchayat
GPF	General Purpose Fund
GST	Goods and Services Tax
IAP	Integrated action plan
IAY	Indira Awas Yojana
ICDS	Integrated Child Development Services
IHSDP	Integrated Housing and Slum Development Programme
IT	Information technology
KMA	Kerala Municipality Act

KPRA	Kerala Panchayat Raj Act
LD	Level of decentralization
LDF	Left Democratic Front
LG	Local government
LSGD	Local Self Government Department
LSGI	Local self-government institution
MC	Municipal corporation
MGNREGA	Mahatma Gandhi National Rural Employment Guarantee Act
MGNREGS	Mahatma Gandhi National Rural Employment Guarantee Scheme
MLA	Member of Legislative Assembly
MPLADS	Member of Parliament Local Area Development Scheme
NABARD	National Bank for Agriculture and Rural Development
NIE	New institutional economics
NIRD	National Institute of Rural Development
NPM	New public management
NRHM	National Rural Health Mission
NUHM	National Urban Health Mission
OECD	Organisation for Economic Co-operation and Development
O&M	Operation and maintenance
PMAY-G	Pradhan Mantri Awas Yojana - Gramin
PRI	Panchayat Raj Institutions
SC	Scheduled Caste
SCP	Special Component Plan
SFC	State Finance Commission
SG	Special grant
SGSY	Swarnajayanti Gram Swarozgar Yojana
SHM	Stakeholders meeting
SJSRY	Swarna Jayanti Shahari Rozgar Yojana
SNG	Sub-national government
SOTR	State own tax revenue
SSA	Sarva Shiksha Abhiyan
ST	Scheduled Tribe

TA	Travelling allowance
TI	Transferred institution
ToR	Terms of reference
TSP	Tribal Sub Plan
UFC	Union Finance Commission
WCP	Women Component Plan

PREFACE

Following the 73rd and 74th Amendments to the Constitution of India and enactment of the Kerala Panchayat Raj Act (KPRA), 1994, and the Kerala Municipality Act (KMA), 1994, Kerala has transferred a number of powers and functions previously exercised by the state government; devolved more state resources to local governments (LGs) and promoted decentralized governance. Besides the traditional civic functions of the local bodies, they have been assigned new functions, such as the transfer of the local-level government institutions such as hospitals, schools and krishi bhavans; maintenance of assets of transferred institutions (TIs); formulation and implementation of annual development plans and a few agency functions. Kerala's radical decentralization and strengthening of the LGs is widely appreciated and acclaimed as a model to be emulated. And the state's decentralized experience of a quarter of a century gives a number of lessons about decentralized governance, local finance, fiscal decentralization and decentralized planning.

The study examines the local finances of rural and urban LGs, fiscal decentralization and decentralized planning in Kerala. The aspects examined are fiscal decentralization and mobilization of own sources of revenue, finances of gram panchayats (GPs), block panchayats (BPs) and district panchayats (DPs), finances of municipalities, intergovernmental fiscal transfers through State Finance Commission (SFC), devolution recommendations of 5th SFC and status of implementation, assessment of decentralized planning of GPs and municipal corporations (MCs).

Major conclusions of the study are the following. The outcome of fiscal decentralization in Kerala is poor or unsatisfactory due to partial and distorted implementation of fiscal decentralization with regard to transfer of taxes and non-tax items, revision of rate of tax and non-tax, implementation of SFC recommendations, dual control of TIs and staff, interference in administration through a host of regulations and controls and entrusting additional agency functions without expansion of administrative machinery and staff.

From Kerala's decentralization and fiscal decentralization experience, we may draw the following lessons. Transfer of a few important functions which are relevant to GPs and municipalities, and which can be executed efficiently with a small administrative set-up, staff, resources, powers, etc., are desirable to be transferred to GPs and municipalities. Transferring a large number of functions at the early stage of decentralization without expanding the administrative machinery and staff, and assignment of more administrative and financial powers will result in poor execution of all the functions. The practice of dual control of the TIs by the state government and LGs is not a sound policy for the efficient functioning of the institutions. Decentralization and transfer of a number of functions including agency functions shall lead to neglect of basic civic functions and consequent poor delivery of civic amenities and services. Partial and distorted fiscal decentralization won't give better fiscal performance of LGs. For better results, the LGs should be given full freedom to levy, collect and effect periodical revision of rate of tax and non-tax items assigned to them. The preconditions for sound intergovernmental transfer of funds are timely constitution of SFCs and prompt implementation of its recommendations. Success in decentralized planning requires dismantling the administrative system, practices, favouring centralized nature of planning and giving freedom to LGs for formulation and execution of projects and plans based on their requirement, priorities and geographic conditions.

Professor M. A. Oommen, Chairman of 4th SFC and an internationally acclaimed expert on decentralization and local governance, has gone through the entire draft of the book and offered a number of valuable comments and suggestions. I have immensely benefited from it. I take this opportunity to express my sincere thanks and gratitude to Professor Oommen.

My experience as Chairman of the 5th SFC has helped me a lot to get a better understanding of fiscal issues of LGs in Kerala and to write this book. I have greatly benefited from discussions with the members of 5th SFC Shri James Varghese IAS, principal secretary, LSGD and Dr V. K. Baby IAS, Special Secretary, Finance Resources, about the complex issues of local governance in Kerala. I got an opportunity to get a clear idea about the ground realities of LGs from my discussions with the mayors of MCs, chairpersons of municipalities and presidents of three-tier panchayats, namely gram, block and district, and secretaries and other officials of LGs belonging to all districts of Kerala during my tenure as chairman of the 5th SFC. Discussions with 5th SFC's officials, especially Shri T. K. Soman, secretary of the Commission, Shri M. Chandra Dhas, consultant, Shri Prathap Kumar, deputy secretary and Shri Abhilash S, assistant section officer about the minute issues of LGs have helped me to get a better understanding of critical issues and problems of LGs in Kerala. Shri Bijil Babu R has provided research support for the book. Shri Raj Madhav Karthik Nair has done the proofreading of the draft. I take this opportunity to express my gratitude to all of them.

B. A. Prakash
Thiruvananthapuram
June 2019

Introduction

INTRODUCTION

The state of Kerala implemented radical decentralization of powers and functions to local governments (LGs) following 73rd and 74th Amendments to the Constitution of India. The amendments gave constitutional status to LGs, established a system of uniform structure, formation of village assemblies or gram sabhas, transfer of 29 subjects to LGs, entrusted responsibility of preparing local area development plans, constitution of district planning committees (DPC), regular elections and transfer of funds from the state government based on the recommendations of State Finance Commissions (SFCs). Constitution of State Election Commission to conduct elections to LGs every five years, reservation of one-third of total seats and chairperson's offices for women, seat reservation for Scheduled Caste (SC) and Scheduled Tribe (ST) population based on their proportion of population, etc., have been implemented. Consequent to the amendments, the State Legislature passed Kerala Panchayat Raj Act (KPRA), 1994, and the Kerala Municipality Act (KMA), 1994, to enable the LGs to function as third tier of government. The State Legislature also amended other related laws to empower LGs. The Acts also envisaged to transfer functions of various departments of the government to LGs.

Between 1995 and 2001, the state government had transferred a number of functions and institutions, and staff to the rural and urban LGs in Kerala. The state government constituted State Election Commission to conduct elections to LGs and SFCs to devolve state taxes and other funds to LGs. High priority was given to decentralized planning and funds were given for financing annual plans of LGs. In the transfer of powers and functions, resource transfer, promotion of decentralized planning, maintenance of assets of the transferred institutions (TIs) and efforts of LGs in the local-level development, Kerala has achieved substantial progress since 1994 compared to other states.

But on some fronts, the performance of LGs has been poor or unsatisfactory. With regard to the execution of civic functions like collection and disposal of solid and liquid waste, control of stray dogs menace, vector control, regulation of slaughtering of animals, maintenance of environmental hygiene, etc., the urban and rural LGs have failed miserably. In spite of the experience of implementation of annual plans for more than two decades, the LGs have not acquired the capacity to formulate or implement annual plan in an efficient or satisfactory manner. The state government has not given powers to LGs to effect periodical revision of the taxes and non-tax items levied and collected by the LGs. Consequently, the rate of taxes, fees, rent, user charges, etc., of majority of the items have remained unchanged for about two decades. Very low priority has been given for own source mobilization by majority of gram panchayats (GPs), municipalities and municipal corporations (MCs). The successive state governments have not implemented majority of the SFC's recommendations, except the item of devolution.

REVIEW OF LITERATURE ON DECENTRALIZATION IN KERALA

A number of attempts were made by scholars, research institutions, government agencies and others to study the decentralized experience of Kerala. The topics studied were decentralization and local governance, decentralized planning, fiscal decentralization, local finance, etc. Among the topics, the largest number of studies were conducted on decentralized planning. Here, we attempt a brief review of literature on decentralization and LGs.

The KPRA, 1994, and KMA, 1994, visualized a partial administrative and fiscal decentralization transferring some functions to rural and urban LGs in a slow and phased manner. But the Left Democratic Front (LDF) government which assumed power in 1996 wanted to implement decentralization as a mass movement and a campaign was started. People's plan campaign, a mass movement, was organized to achieve the rapid local-level development through decentralized planning (Thomas Isaac and Franke 2000; Thomas Isaac and Harilal 1997). Like a literacy movement, the campaign was aimed to educate about the benefits of decentralized planning to various sections like elected representatives of LGs, officials, retired officials interested in LGs, members of gram sabhas, people's organization, etc. It is believed that through discussions in gram sabhas, development seminar organized by LGs, training of resource persons, constitution of task forces to prepare projects, etc., one can create favourable conditions to prepare development plans most suited to local conditions. The state government decided to allot about one-third of plan funds of the state for the plans of local bodies.

An unattainable target of 25 per cent of total resources of the plans of local bodies was aimed to be mobilized through voluntary labour and contribution from the public. An illusion was created that all the problems related to the local-level development will be solved through the decentralized planning. Though unprecedented publicity was given about the plan campaign, no serious attempts were made to the change administrative machinery, provision of adequate staff, enhancing the capabilities of elected representatives to manage the affairs, changes in the procedures of administration, plan formulation, monitoring and execution, etc. This had resulted in hasty implementation of the plan, lot of wasteful expenditure of plan funds for benefit distribution schemes, neglect of infrastructure projects and poor achievement of financial and physical targets in the first year of implementation of decentralized planning (Prakash 1999). The measures taken for the promotion of decentralized planning during the second half of the 1990s are discussed in other works (Thomas Isaac and Franke 2000; Thomas Isaac and Heller 2003).

Following the implementation of decentralized governance in LGs, a number of attempts were made to study the different aspects of the decentralization. The India Panchayat Raj Report is one of the earliest studies which provides a fairly good assessment on the progress made in decentralization in Panchayat Raj Institutions (PRI) in

Indian states during the second half of the 1990s (National Institute of Rural Development 2001). The study concluded that the states had not devolved powers and functions on the PRIs in accordance with the spirit of the 73rd Constitutional Amendment. The mandatory, civic functions, implementation of pension and welfare schemes and maintenance of assets of the GPs in Kerala were examined in a study based on the data collected from a sample of 50 GPs (Prakash 2005b). The study came to the conclusion that with the decentralization, there had been an unprecedented increase in the mandatory, civic, plan and welfare functions and administrative work, but no corresponding increase in the number of staff or expansion in administrative machinery or procedures in administration leading to poor performance on all fronts.

The decentralized planning experience in Kerala was widely discussed in the country during the 2000s and a number of scholars have examined different aspects of the same. Comparing the experiences of decentralized planning in West Bengal and Kerala, a study arrived at the conclusion that Kerala's participatory planning was superior to West Bengal in many respects (Charvak 2000). Some of the studies examined plan campaign, its relevance, participatory nature, democratic character, involvement of people in planning process, merits of transfer of plan functions to LGs, process of plan formulation at the local level, etc. (Chathukulam and John 2002; Mohanakumar 2002, 2003; Raghuram 2000; Sharma 2003). These studies gave overemphasis to the merits of decentralized planning, which was at the infant stage, projected it as an institutional change required to solve the economic backwardness of rural areas in Indian context and failed to provide an analysis of demerits, limitations and problems created due to the transformation.

The other notable studies which examined decentralized planning are the following. A study which examined functioning of elected representatives and presidents in Madhya Pradesh, Kerala and Tamil Nadu came to the conclusion that Kerala's position was much better (Narayana 2005). Another study on the plan campaign based on a sample survey of 72 panchayats came to the conclusion that campaign devolved new authority and resources to panchayats and mandated structures and processes designed to maximize the direct involvement of citizens in planning and budgeting (Heller, Harilal and Chaudhari 2007).

The merits and demerits of decentralized planning are pointed out in the official evaluation studies. The Planning Commission's evaluation study on decentralized planning in Kerala came to the conclusion that productive sector projects of LGs did not develop in to a comprehensive plan mainly due to inadequate capacity of LGs to formulate productive sector projects. Absence of integration between the plans of GPs, BPs and DPs, preoccupation of gram sabhas with distribution of various items of benefits, inadequate maintenance funds for maintaining the assets created, lack of expertise in plan formulation and implementation, and lack of coordination between the functionaries in plan formulation and implementation had contributed to poor plan performance (Planning Commission 2006). The committee on evaluation of decentralized planning found that the overall growth performance during the post-decentralization period was very good. The state achieved substantial progress in provision of basic minimum needs, pro-poor expenditure and development of infrastructural facility. But the demerits are ward-wise distribution of funds, plans emerging from negotiated priorities, ineffective working groups and technical advisory groups, poor spending of Special Component Plan (SCP) and Tribal Sub Plan (TSP) funds, failure of DPs to prepare district level plans, etc. (Government of Kerala 2009).

We may examine the literature on fiscal decentralization, devolution of resources and local finances. Kerala's fiscal decentralization experience was examined by the World Bank with an objective to determine an acceptable fiscal devolution package for India (Oommen 2004). The study concluded that the expenditure of local bodies, particularly the GPs, indicates that the local-level development activity has received impetus in Kerala. But much remains to be done to institutionalize effective fiscal decentralization. Revenue mobilization can be significantly enhanced by better tax effort and tax reforms. An examination of fiscal decentralization experience of major states in India for a decade found that the fiscal scenario is disturbing (Oommen 2006). There has been a decline in the percentage of LG expenditure in relation to the total government expenditure, and average rate of growth in tax revenue of urban and rural local bodies in most states registered a negative trend. Another study on fiscal decentralization came to the conclusion that urban local bodies are better placed than rural regarding degree of fiscal autonomy and fiscal decentralization in India (Srivastava 2008). The study says that Kerala has effectively implemented fiscal decentralization compared to other states in India.

The institution mandated to effect devolution of resources to LGs is SFC. The five SFCs which were constituted to devolve state taxes and other funds to LGs have used different approaches to fiscal devolution (State Finance Commission 1996, 2001, 2005, 2011, 2015, 2016). Among them, the second Commission had put forward a norm of devolution for meeting on expenditure on general purpose, maintenance and development (State Finance Commission 2001). The 5th SFC has deviated from the earlier norms of devolution and recommended a share of state own tax revenue (SOTR) for general purpose, maintenance and development on the basis of SOTR received in the year of devolution and changed the norms of allocation of maintenance fund and Union Finance Commission (UFC) grant (State Finance Commission 2015, 2016).

A major gap in literature is the lack of studies on the finances of different categories of rural and urban LGs. The only exception is the one which examined the financial sources, fiscal impact of increase in transfers and the need for evolving reliable and stable financial reporting systems of GPs in Kerala (Oommen, Wallace and Muwonge 2017). The study arrived at the conclusion that the pressure to spend on welfare and development activities has outstripped the growth in revenue and that the LGs have not utilized their revenue potential.

The review of literature on decentralization in Kerala can be concluded as follows. The researchers gave too much emphasis on decentralized planning and too little on other aspects of decentralization. The state lacks literature on most of the other aspects of decentralization and governance, constraints and problems faced by the LGs, etc. There is a serious gap in the literature on finances of different categories of urban and rural LGs. This is the context in which the study is attempted.

CATEGORY OF LOCAL GOVERNMENTS

Kerala has two categories of LGs, namely rural having three-tier panchayats consisting of gram, block and district, and urban consisting of municipalities and MCs. Table 1.1 gives growth in the number of LGs between 1995 and 2015.

A structural change that has been occurring in the state is the decline in number of GPs (village panchayats) and increase in number of urban LGs since 2010. The number of municipalities has increased from 53 in 2005 to 87 in 2015. This is largely due to the rapid urbanization that has been taking place in the state. The share of urban population according to the Census has increased from 25.9 per cent in 2001 to 47.7 per cent in 2011. In November 2015, a new MC, namely Kannur, was formed. The other MCs are Thiruvananthapuram, Kollam, Kochi, Thrissur and Kozhikode (State Finance Commission 2015).

We may examine the number of wards in rural and urban LGs. A ward is a constituency from which a member of the three-tier panchayat or a councillor of the municipality or MCs is elected by the voters of the ward. Table 1.2 presents the number of wards of rural and urban LGs in 2010 and 2015.

The average area and population of rural and urban LGs is given in Table 1.3.

Table 1.1 *Number of Rural and Urban LGs in Kerala from 1995 to 2015*

LG	1995	2000	2005	2010	2015
		Rural			
GP	990	991	999	978	941
BP	152	152	152	152	152
DP	14	14	14	14	14
		Urban			
Municipality	55	53	53	60	87
MC	3	5	5	5	6
Total	**1,214**	**1,215**	**1,223**	**1,209**	**1,200**

Source: State Finance Commission 2015.

Table 1.2 *Number of Wards of LGs in Kerala*

LG	2010			2015 (as on November)		
	Number of LGs	Number of Wards	Average Number	Number of LGs	Number of Wards	Average Number
Rural						
GP	978	16,680	17	941	15,962	17
BP	152	2,095	14	152	2,076	14
DP	14	332	24	14	331	24
Urban						
Municipalities	60	2,216	37	87	3,122	36
MCs	5	359	72	6	414	69
Total	**1,209**	**21,682**	–	**1,200**	**21,905**	–

Source: State Finance Commission 2015.

Table 1.3 *Average Area and Population of LGs in 2011*

LG	Number	Average Area (Sq. km.)	Average Population (2011 Census)
DPs	14	2,651.7	1,903,357
BPs	152	244.24	175,309
GPs	978	37.16	26,674
MCs	5	95.6	491,240
Municipalities	60	23.65	51,664
Total	**1,209**	–	–

Source: State Finance Commission 2015.

A district-wise distribution of LGs is given in Table 1.4. Malappuram district has the largest number of GPs followed by Palakkad, Thrissur and Ernakulam districts. On the other hand, Wayanad district has the lowest number of GPs. Ernakulum is a highly urbanized district having 13 municipalities. Malappuram district is the second district having largest number of municipalities. On the other hand, Idukki district is the least urbanized district having only 2 municipalities. The major MCs in the state are Thiruvananthapuram, Kochi and Kozhikode.

Table 1.4 *District-Wise Distribution of LGs (as on 1 November 2015; in Number)*

District	GPs	BPs	DPs	Municipalities	MCs
Thiruvananthapuram	73	11	1	4	1
Kollam	68	11	1	4	1
Pathanamthitta	53	8	1	4	0
Alappuzha	72	12	1	6	0
Kottayam	71	11	1	6	0
Idukki	52	8	1	2	0
Ernakulam	82	14	1	13	1
Thrissur	86	16	1	7	1
Palakkad	88	13	1	7	0
Malappuram	94	15	1	12	0
Kozhikode	70	12	1	7	1
Wayanad	23	4	1	3	0
Kannur	71	11	1	9	1
Kasargod	38	6	1	3	0
Total	**941**	**152**	**14**	**87**	**6**

Source: State Finance Commission 2015.

OBJECTIVES, HYPOTHESES AND DATA SOURCES

We have seen that a major gap in literature is there on studies on fiscal decentralization, mobilization of own source of revenue and finances of different categories of rural and urban LGs. This is the context in which the study is attempted.

1. To examine fiscal decentralization and mobilization of own source of revenue.
2. To analyse finances of rural LGs (GPs), block panchayats (BPs) and district panchayats (DPs) and municipalities.
3. To discuss SFC's recommendations on devolution of resources.
4. To examine the decentralized planning and plan performance.

We present the following hypotheses to explain fiscal decentralization and mobilization of own source revenue, finances of different categories of LGs, SFC's recommendations and decentralized planning performance.

1. The outcome of fiscal decentralization in Kerala is poor or unsatisfactory due to partial and distorted implementation of fiscal decentralization with regard to transfer of taxes and non-tax items, revision of rate of tax and non-tax, implementation of SFC recommendations, dual control of TIs and staff, interference in administration through a host of regulations and controls, and entrusting additional agency functions without expansion of administrative machinery and staff.

2. The fiscal policy of non-transfer of new taxes to LGs, non-transfer of powers to revise rates or effect periodical revision of tax and non-tax items; failure of successive state governments to effect periodical revision of rates of taxes and non-tax items collected by LGs and low priority given by LGs for own resource mobilization have contributed to poor own resource mobilization and heavy reliance on transferred funds by LGs.

3. Though core functions of GPs, municipalities and MCs are mandatory, civic and development, the assignment of additional agency functions like distribution of welfare pensions, implementation of CSS, etc., without expanding the administrative machinery and staff, has resulted in the deterioration of its civic functions like waste disposal, controlling stray dogs, running slaughter houses, etc., and plan performance of development plans.

4. Though Kerala's fiscal transfers through SFCs has certain merits, namely timely constitution, fiscal devolution based on norms, somewhat sufficient transfer of funds to meet their functions; the demerits such as delayed implementation of SFC reports, implementation of a small share of recommendations, non-implementation of most of the recommendations other than devolution, refusing to implement accepted recommendations, under some pretext, outweigh the merits.

5. The causes for the poor plan performance of urban and rural LGs can be attributed to factors such as irrational and irrelevant plan

formulation guidelines giving too much emphasis for pre-project preparation formalities, an unsuitable and uniform plan guidelines meant for all categories of LGs, non-functioning working groups, low priority and very little time given for actual project preparations, implementation of a large and unmanageable number of projects, splitting projects into tiny projects giving undue importance to wards, delays in getting approvals and entrusting work, entrusting execution of majority of projects to incompetent beneficiary committees, inadequate engineers and supporting staff, delayed execution of projects, bunching of plan expenditure to last quarter or last month and restrictions imposed on passing bills due to treasury restrictions.

Data Source

The data for the study were collected from a sample of all categories of LGs using a structured schedule. Financial data were collected from a sample of 56 GPs belonging to all districts, 13 BPs, 13 DPs and 14 municipalities. Besides this, we have used the data from the 5th SFC reports. For examining the plan performance of GPs and municipalities, we have used the data of the 5th SFC. The 5th SFC has collected large volume of data from all categories of urban and rural LGs, government departments, government agencies concerned with the activities of LGs and other stakeholders. We have also used these data for the study.

Fiscal Decentralization

2

Theoretical Issues

In this chapter, we will discuss the conceptual and theoretical issues of LG and local governance, decentralization and fiscal decentralization.

LOCAL GOVERNMENT AND LOCAL GOVERNANCE

The definition given by Anwar Shah gives a fairly good idea about the concept of LG and local governance.

Local government refers to specific institutions or entities created by national or State constitutions, ordinary legislation of a higher level of central government, provincial or State legislation, or by executive order to deliver a range of specified services to a relatively small geographically delineated area.

Local governance is a broader concept and is defined as the formulation and execution of collective action at the local level. Thus it encompasses the direct and indirect roles of formal institutions of LG and government hierarchies, as well as the roles of informal norms, networks, community organisations, and neighbourhood associations in pursuing collective action by defining the framework for citizen-citizen and citizen-State interactions, collective decision making, and delivery of local public services. (Shah 2006)

In a broader perspective, local governance is not simply to provide a range of local services but to preserve life and liberty of people, creating space for democratic participation and civic dialogue, promotion of sustainable local development and aiming at enhancing the welfare of the people.

Roles of LG: Analytical Perspectives

To discuss the roles and responsibilities of LGs, six analytical perspectives are presented, namely (a) traditional fiscal federalism, (b) new public management (NPM), (c) public choice, (d) new institutional economics (NIE), (e) network forms of local governance and (f) citizen-centred governance (Shah 2006). The traditional fiscal federalism approach considers LG as a subordinate tier in a multi-tiered system and puts forth principles for defining the roles and responsibilities of orders of government. Here, subject to the constitutional and legal status of LGs, state governments in federal countries assume varying degrees of oversight of the provision of local public services.

The literature on NPM perspectives discusses what LGs should do and how they should do it better. It is assumed that citizens are the main actors but they also perform multiple roles as governors (voters, owner–authorizers, taxpayers, community members), activist–producers (providers of services, self-helpers obliging others to act, co-producers) and consumers (clients and beneficiaries). Emphasis is given to the government as an agent of the people, entrusted with serving public interest and creating public value. Public value is defined as measurable improvements in social outcomes or quality of life. It is also argued that LGs utilize some of the resources that come as free goods—namely resources of goodwill, consent, contributions in cash and kind, compliance, community spirit and collective public action, instead of diverting resources from the private sector. The NPM approach advocates for creating an environment for managers that not only gives them flexibility in the use of resources but also holds them accountable for results. It is argued for discarding top-down controls and replacing it with bottom-up focus on results.

The literature on public choice supports the self-interest doctrine of government, arguing that it is expected of the various stakeholders involved in policy formulation and implementation that they would use opportunities and resources to advance their self-interest. The bearing of such a view on the design of LG institutions is immense. LGs must have complete local autonomy in taxing and spending, and they must be subject to competition within and beyond government for them to serve the interests of people. The assumptions underlying this approach are the following: (a) an LG that assumes it has complete knowledge and acts to maximize the welfare of its residents, (b) an LG that provides services in accordance with local residents' willingness to pay, (c) an LG that stresses on public service provision to further social objectives and (d) an LG that is dominated by self-interested bureaucrats and politicians.

The NIE framework views the various orders of government (as agents) being created to serve the interests of the people as citizens, with the jurisdictional design being such as to ensure that these agents (various orders of government) serve the public interest while minimizing transaction costs for the principals (citizens). The information asymmetry prevailing in the existing institutional framework prevents such optimization as the agents (various orders of government) are having greater information than the principals (citizens), owing to the higher transaction cost that the latter must incur to obtain information, making the contract between the two incomplete and thereby creating an environment that fosters commitment problems on the part of the agents. It is in this light that the NIE attains relevance, as it emphasizes on designing jurisdictions based on various elements of transaction costs for various services and in evaluating choices between competing governance mechanisms.

Given the multiplicity of organizations involved in local governance, coordination among them is highly critical for successful local governance. With the market (wherein a contract management agency enters into a binding contract with all partners) and hierarchical (wherein institutional arrangements are made to clarify roles and responsibilities and to establish mechanism for consultation, coordination and cooperation) mechanisms entailing high transaction costs and perceived infeasibility, a network form of governance has been suggested as a mode of governance for such partnerships. The network would be managed by LGs and could be formed based on shared interests (interest-based networks) or hope-based networks which are built on shared sentiments and emotions of members.

Citizen-centred local governance approach advocates reforming the institutions of local governance which requires agreement on the following basic principles, namely responsive governance, responsible governance and accountable governance. *Responsive governance* implies that the services delivered are in line with the citizens' preferences. *Responsible governance* requires that the government must be prudent in managing its fiscal resources. It should seek to improve the public services in terms of its quantity and quality as well as the access to such services. This can be achieved by benchmarking its performance with the best performing LGs. *Accountable governance* implies that the LG must be accountable to its citizens or electorate. Appropriate safeguards must be adhered to by the LGs to ensure that public interest is served by it with integrity. These basic principles make up the framework of citizen-centred governance. The framework has the following significant features, namely (a) empowering the citizens via a rights-based approach that includes provisions for direct democracy which would require referenda to be held on important government decisions thereby giving citizens the right to veto any legislation or government programme, citizens' charter that would outline the citizens' basic rights as well as their rights of access to specific standards of public services; (b) bottom-up accountability that would make governance more result oriented; (c) evaluation of government performance in its role of being a facilitator of a network of providers by citizens. Hence, this framework stresses on reforms that enhance the role of citizens as principals and create incentives to government agents to act in accordance with their mandates.

Changing Governance Structure

Radical changes have been taking place in governance structure in the 21st century compared to the previous century. According to Anwar Shah, a silent revolution had been taking place in the world where there was a shift from a centralized governance structure to a globalized and localized one in the 21st century (Table 2.1).

The role of the central government in such an environment has been changing from a managerial authority to a leadership. The culture of

Table 2.1 *Governance Structure 20th Century versus 21st Century*

20th Century	21st Century
Unitary	Federal/confederal
Centralized	Globalized and localized
Centre manages	Centre leads
Bureaucratic	Participatory
Command and control	Responsive and accountable to citizens
Input controls	Results matter
Top-down accountability	Bottom-up accountability
Internally dependent	Competitive
Closed and slow	Open and quick
Intolerance of risk	Freedom to fail/succeed

Source: Shah (2004).

governance is slowly changing from bureaucratic to a participatory approach; from command and control to accountability of results. The transformation has been from top-down accountability mode to bottom-up accountability mode; internally dependent to competitive and closed economy to open economy. It is pointed out that the overall thrust of these changes accelerate a process of decentralization in the powers and functions of governments to the local level. And localization can be achieved through varying combination of political, administrative and fiscal decentralization measures.

LGs in Developing Countries: A Review

A review of LGs in developing countries such as South Africa, Kazakhstan, Chile, India, Argentina, Indonesia, Brazil, China, Poland and Uganda reveals that they follow the traditional roles of local governance and simply provide a narrow range of local services directly (Shah 2006). The review found that except for a couple of countries such as Brazil, China and Poland, the role of LGs in people's lives continues to be limited. They typically are bounded by the principle of ultra vires and are permitted to discharge only a small number of functions, which are mandated from earlier. Their autonomy in expenditure decisions is limited and has hardly any autonomy in revenue raising decisions. For own source revenues, their access is constrained to a few non-productive bases. Bureaucratic and political leaders at the local level are more interested in seeking higher levels of fiscal transfers than in lobbying for more taxing powers. Political and expenditure decentralization have raced ahead of tax decentralization. In developing countries, fiscal transfers account for 60 per cent of revenues (51% in sample developing countries), whereas in Organisation for Economic Co-operation and Development (OECD) countries, the corresponding figure is 34 per cent. The design of fiscal transfers remains flawed in most of the countries, even in the presence of formula-driven fiscal transfers opted by most of them. No incentives are created by these transfers for setting national minimum standards or accountability for results and typically also do not serve the objectives of regional fiscal equity. The autonomy enjoyed by LGs in hiring and firing LG employees is also limited.

DECENTRALIZATION

A number of definitions were used to define the concept of decentralization based on the experiences and approach of decentralization of different countries and their political interests. Some of the definitions used for the analysis of decentralization are given further.

> The term 'decentralization' implies the transfer of responsibility and competence to democratically independent lower levels of government. This term is to be viewed as opposed to the term 'deconcentration' that implies transfer of responsibility from central ministries to field officers at the local or regional level, thereby becoming closer to the citizens while remaining part of the central government'. (Bird, Ebel and Wallice 1995)

> 'Decentralisation' is defined as 'devolution' of power to independent sub-national governments (SNGs), which are given responsibilities for determining the level and quality of service to be provided, the manner in which those services will be provided and the source and types of funds to finance the delivery of those service. (Steffensen and Trollegaard 2000)

The complex phenomenon of decentralization can be classified into three types: deconcentration, delegation and devolution. In deconcentration, the decision-making power is with higher level government, and the lower level is merely employed to implement the higher level's policies and programmes. In delegation, the higher level government delegates decision-making power to the lower level for specified functions. Only in devolution is decision-making power shared between the higher and lower levels of government, so that genuine decentralization is evident. Such a concept has administrative, political and fiscal dimensions. The effectiveness of decentralization requires the calibration of these three independent dimensions. The political component refers to the transfer of authority from central to local authorities, the administrative component speaks of the transfer of functional responsibilities from central to local authorities and the fiscal component addresses to the financial relationship between all levels of government (World Bank 2004).

> Decentralisation is often advocated by many, particularly the international donor agencies, for its unique potentiality for improving the delivery of public services at the local level. But, that is the instrumental value of local democracy. We may define decentralization as the empowerment of the common people through the empowerment of the LGs. (Oommen 2009)

This definition gives autonomy as the essence of empowerment and in empowering and building the capabilities of LGs, five aspects are crucial in a federal system. One, autonomy with reference to assigned functions. Two, fiscal decentralization is a logical corollary of functional devolution. Three, administrative autonomy. Four, critical aspect of decentralization may be referred to as institutional decentralization. It is important that all major institutions that have a direct bearing on the functions devolved must be transferred to the appropriate level of government. The fifth aspect refers to responsiveness. Decisions that an LG make should reflect the felt needs of the community.

The World Bank gives an analytical framework to analyse the process of decentralization as follows. 'Decentralization is a multi-faceted process which includes giving discretion to LGs and establishing accountability mechanisms at three different levels of governance—political, administrative and fiscal' (World Bank 2009). The key elements of the analytical framework of decentralization are the following: (a) decentralization reforms grant LGs new powers and responsibilities in three dimensions: political, administrative and fiscal. These dimensions provide discretionary space to LGs; (b) ensuring appropriate use of such discretionary space requires introducing effective accountability systems. Within their discretionary space, LGs would be accountable to higher levels of government (upward accountability) as well as to citizens (downward accountability); (c) public accountability mechanisms safeguard against misuse and abuse of local discretion, but they have imperfections. Hence, new forms of social accountability mechanisms are required; (d) public and social accountability approaches must be bridged to ensure that citizens have the ability and opportunity to demand accountability.

Decentralization Reforms: Country Experiences

The World Bank has conducted a study to evaluate decentralization reforms in 10 different countries using the aforementioned framework and arrived at the following conclusions (World Bank 2009). The countries studied are Angola, Tanzania, Rwanda, Guinea, Burkina Faso, India (Kerala), Pakistan (Punjab), Ethiopia, the Philippines and Uganda. The main findings of the study are the following: (a) significant variations exist in terms of sequencing of reforms in political, administrative and fiscal domains. Depending on the intended outcomes and the interests of the political leadership, the sequencing varies; (b) decentralization reforms in many contexts failed to create a more participatory environment at the local level. Democratic decentralization reforms have rarely remained true to their purpose of creating empowered democratic local authorities; (c) discretion and accountability relationships depend on the political economy of each country, historical/colonial legacies and the level of trust that exists between government and citizens; (d) even in countries with highly developed rules and regulations, significant gap exists between de jure and de facto practices. A significant discrepancy between laws and practices exists mainly due to lack of sufficient incentives for both central and local authorities to implement laws and lack of sufficient capacity to carry out the newly assigned roles and responsibilities; (e) in majority of the countries, decentralization reforms are not well designed to bridge discretion and accountability. In none of the cases analysed, decentralization reforms were able to link discretion and accountability and bridge supply- and demand-side approaches; (f) not all public services present a very good case for decentralization; (g) there is confusion in roles and responsibilities among the relevant decentralized bodies and actors, which adversely impacts accountability structures; (h) social accountability mechanisms by themselves are not sustainable; integrating mechanisms of upward and downward accountability is essential for improving service delivery performance; (i) assessing local institutional capacities is fundamental to determine an appropriate mix of decentralization. It is lack of capacity, in addition to lack of incentives, which acts as a huge constraint to well-designed decentralization; (j) the study concludes that providing discretionary power to LGs and strengthening their accountability towards citizens are necessary strategies for an effective implementation of decentralization reforms. At the same time, a number of other operational changes like strengthening the LGs by providing training, better engagement of central governments with LGs, attention towards all three aspects of decentralization, etc., can improve the implementation of a well-designed decentralization system.

FISCAL DECENTRALIZATION

'Fiscal decentralization is primarily concerned with implementing an effective intergovernmental fiscal system. Intergovernmental fiscal rules determine expenditure responsibilities and revenue resources of LGs as well as the design of intergovernmental transfers system and LGs' access to capital markets' (Bird 2000). According to Bird, fiscal decentralization is based on four pillars: expenditure assignment, revenue assignment, intergovernmental transfers/grants and sub-national debt/borrowing; (a) assignment of expenditure responsibilities refers to the distribution of functions among the different government levels. It improves the responsiveness of the LGs to the local preference, enhances accountability and avoids unproductive overlap, duplication of authority and legal challenges; (b) allocating own source revenue refers to the distribution of financial resources among the different levels of government. It ensures sub-national autonomy, promotes accountability and ownership, realizes decentralization efficiency gains and facilitates cash flow management; (c) the intergovernmental fiscal transfers refer to the transfer of finances from the central government to lower government levels. In general, the revenue assignment never matches the expenditure needs, so intergovernmental fiscal transfers are often necessary to assure revenue adequacy. It ensures bridging the vertical fiscal gap, improve horizontal fiscal balance, fund national priorities, compensate for spillovers or externalities, etc., (d) local borrowing for sub-national governments (SNGs) stands as the fourth pillar of fiscal decentralization and can act as a major source of revenue for the LG, especially in countries where own source revenue and intergovernmental transfers are deficient with respect to local investment requirements.

Fiscal Decentralization Policy Design

Scholars have put forward the components of a system of fiscal decentralization, its sub-components, the steps of sequencing of fiscal decentralization and arguments for fiscal decentralization (Bahl and Vazquez 2005). A summary of the points of the policy design for fiscal decentralization is given further (Table 2.2).

Intergovernmental fiscal relations must be considered as a system and all the pieces in the system must fit together. The implementation of a decentralization programme should ideally begin with a design of the comprehensive system and should lay out the plan for each element of the system.

Determinants of Local Fiscal Decentralization

The major determinants of local fiscal decentralization are defining the role of LGs in service delivery and assignment of expenditure, revenue assignment to finance service delivery, financing fiscal gap through

Table 2.2 *The Components of a System of Fiscal Decentralization*

Component	Desirable Feature
Representation	Popular election of executive and legislative branches
Chief officers	Locally appointed
Expenditure discretion	Significant control over how money is spent
Budget	Local approval; hard budget constraint
Revenue	Significant local power: discretion to change rates in a closed list of taxes
Intergovernmental equalization Transfers	Unconditional and formula driven
Conditional, specific purpose	Block grants using formulas or other objective allocations; matching
Borrowing powers	Broad borrowing powers and hard budget constraint
Civil service	Locals hire, fire and determine compensation

intergovernmental transfer system and assignment of borrowing powers to LGs (World Bank 2009). First, as the main goal of decentralization is to improve the responsiveness of the LG to local preferences, devolving expenditure responsibilities for the public goods to LGs is the major step of decentralization. The ability of the LG to fulfil this depends on the extent of discretion available to the LG to make their own expenditure allocation decisions for local public goods with necessary reporting, monitoring and sanctioning of this expenditure. Second, own source revenue is the most important source of revenue for the LG to finance its activities due to the following reasons; (a) there are no strings attached to own source revenues and, hence, it improves the ability of the LG to be more responsive to the citizens; (b) own source revenue enables the government to bunch each expenditure along with a tax to finance it. Such a bunching would enable the voters to assess the performance of their elected representatives in terms of the quantities and qualities of government services they are getting for the taxes they pay and (c) own source revenue would ensure that allocative efficiency is maintained by ensuring that the LG equates cost and benefit at the margin. This is in stark contrast to when costs can be shifted to central budgets which would lead to LGs not making the most efficient decisions.

Third, intergovernmental transfers are an essential component of fiscal decentralization. The assignment of revenue and expenditure gives rise to vertical imbalances, that is, the mismatch between revenue sources and expenditure needs of LGs. As total elimination of vertical imbalance is impossible as some degree of discrepancy between expenditure needs and revenue capacity is unavoidable, intergovernmental transfers may redress this vertical imbalance. In designing a transfer system, the first step is to determine the total amount of resources to be transferred to the LGs, that is, establishing the size of the distributable pool. The total amount of transfers may be determined in three ways: (a) rule-based fixed percentage share of dedicated revenues; (b) ad hoc (normally as part of annual budget decision) and (c) as a proportion of approved specific local expenditures to be reimbursed. Of the three, the rule-based transfer system brings greater stability and predictability, and hence promotes good planning and efficient service delivery effort. The next step is to distribute the pool among LGs. Four general mechanisms are utilized for distribution, namely (a) revenue allocation based on jurisdictions where they were collected or the derivation principle; (b) ad hoc/discretionary; (c) formulae based on pre-specified variables and (d) reimbursement of costs. Generally, distribution of funds by formulae or derivation principle is the most effective system. Fourth, local borrowing stands as another component of intergovernmental fiscal system and can act as a major source of revenue for the LG, especially in countries where own source revenue and intergovernmental transfers are deficient with respect to local investment requirements.

Recent Trends in Fiscal Decentralization in Developing Economies

Recent studies reveal that in the case of developing and transition economies (DTEs), there has been a shift from centralized path of governance to decentralized one with emphasis on fiscal decentralization

(Shah 2004). A number of recent developments, discussed further, are prompting most DTEs to re-examine the respective roles of levels of government and opt for decentralization. The important reasons attributed to this development are: (a) the collapse of economies with collective ownership and control; (b) desire to break away from the vestiges of colonialism and ethnic strife as in Africa; (c) central government failures in securing national objectives; (d) beggar-thy-neighbour and fend-for-yourself federalism policies of SNGs; (e) assertion of basic rights of citizens by the courts; (f) globalization of economic activities and (g) the demonstration effects of European Union and Latin America. The vision of governance is gradually indicating a shift from unitary constitutional structures to federal or confederal form of governance for a large majority of the people. It implies that we are likely to move to a globalized and localized world from a centralized one. The overall thrust of these changes manifest as a trend towards either devolution (empowering people politically) and/or localization (decentralization of decision-making to the local level). Political, administrative and fiscal decentralization initiatives have been utilized in pursuing localization.

Fiscal Decentralization in Developing and Transition Economy

The World Bank has presented a few decentralization indicators and examined the progress of fiscal decentralization in DTEs. The indicators are sub-national expenditure as percentage of gross domestic product (GDP), public sector expenditure and public sector education expenditure, public sector health expenditure. The sub-national revenues as percentage of GDP, fiscal transfer, tax and expenditure autonomy are also used as indicators. The results of the study are presented in Table 2.3. It was found that in the case of education expenditure, revenue, tax and expenditure autonomy, the transition economies were in a better position compared to developing economies. On the other hand, with regard to public sector health expenditure and fiscal transfers, the developing countries are better placed.

Table 2.3 *Fiscal Decentralization Indicators*

	Transition Economies (1999)	Developing Economies (1997)
	Average	
Sub-national Expenditures		
As % of GDP	10.8	7.4
As % of public sector expenditures	22.3	23.3
Sub-national education expenditures, as % of public sector education expenditures	55.9	49.8
Sub-national health expenditure, as % of public sector health expenditures	41.9	60.2
Sub-national Revenues		
As % of GDP	7.9	5.3
As % of public sector revenues	18.4	16.6
Fiscal Transfers		
As % of sub-national revenues	24.0	42.2
Sub-national Autonomy		
Tax autonomy	55.1	40.1
Expenditure autonomy	74.0	58.0

Source: Shah (2004).

The study also examined the involvement of central government in certain local functions like social services, transportations, utility services, etc. (Table 2.4). According to the study, waste collection was the major function of LGs in 93 per cent of the countries. Urban highways and urban transportation were the other important functions of the LGs in majority of the countries. In more than one-third of the countries, fire protection, and primary and secondary education were the functions of LGs. On the other hand, public health, hospitals, drinking water, sewerage, electric power supply and police were the functions of central or provisional governments in the sample countries.

Table 2.4 *Central Involvement in Local Functions*

Public Service		Number of Countries				
		Purely Central Function	Central Government Involvement (Other)	Purely Local Function	Sample Size (Total)	Purely Local to Total (%)
Social services	Primary and preschool education	12	9	12	33	36.36
	Secondary education	13	8	10	31	32.26
	Public health	9	14	8	31	25.81
	Hospitals	11	12	4	27	14.81
Transportation	Urban highways	7	5	17	29	58.62
	Urban transportation	6	4	12	22	54.55
Utility services	Drinking water and sewerage	8	16	6	30	20
	Waste collection	0	2	27	29	93.10
	Electric power supply	8	13	4	25	16.00
Other services	Fire protection	0	5	4	9	44.45
	Public order and safety	1	1	0	2	0
	Police	14	10	5	29	17.24

Source: Shah (2004).

A study of the fiscal decentralization experiences of 33 developing and transition countries gives us the following conditions for sound fiscal decentralization (Shah 2004).

Preconditions for Sound Fiscal Decentralization

The important conditions required for a sound fiscal decentralization system of an LG are the following: (a) clear assignment of functions and expenditure responsibilities; (b) allocation of own source revenue and powers to levy collect and revise taxes, fees, user charges, etc., assigned to LGs; (c) unconditional and formula-driven intergovernmental transfers to cover the gap in resources between own resources and expenditure; (d) powers to borrow funds for meeting current and capital items of expenditure; (e) powers to prepare budgets and conduct fiscal operations based on it; (g) powers to appoint staff, initiate disciplinary actions and terminate services; (h) public accountability mechanisms such as audit of accounts by public authority to safeguard against misuse and abuse of local discretion; (i) social accountability mechanisms where the citizens or civil society organizations can demand accountability of the LGs and better service delivery.

Indicators of Fiscal Decentralization

Some indicators of fiscal decentralization are proposed to measure level of decentralization (LD), level of autonomy, criteria of distribution, financial regulation, tax potential, tax autonomy, expenditure autonomy, etc. Table 2.5 gives some of the indicators used to measure fiscal decentralization. The indicators will help us to find out the LD, level of fiscal autonomy, tax autonomy, expenditure autonomy, etc.

Table 2.5 *Indicators of Fiscal Decentralization*

No	Indicator	Measuring FD/Fiscal Changes
1	Share of SNG expenditure of total public expenditure	LD (high, medium and low)
2	Share of SNG recurrent expenditure of total public expenditure	LD
3	Share of SNG capital expenditure of total public capital expenditure	LD
4	Share of SNG revenues of total public revenues	LD
5	Share of SNG expenditures of GDP	LD
6	SNG possibility for SNG borrowing (potential/actual)	Borrowing potential
7	Wage share of the total SNG recurrent expenses	Relationship between wages and investment
8	Share of general public services expenses of total SNG recurrent expenses	Nature of administration
9	Share of capital SNG expenses of total SNG expenses	Development of infrastructure and service provision
10	Share of own revenue sources total SNG revenues	Level of autonomy
11	Appropriate system of transfers from central government	Criteria of distribution
12	Existence of a financial system to regulate for transfer of tasks between the levels	Financial regulation
13	Non-utilization of revenue potential	Efficiency of tax potential
14	Assignment of tax autonomy	Tax autonomy
15	Autonomy on current expenditures	Expenditure autonomy
16	Autonomy on the capital expenditures	Autonomy of capital expenditures

Source: Steffensen and Trollengaard (2000).

Fiscal Decentralization and Mobilization of Own Source of Revenue

INTRODUCTION

This chapter presents an analysis of fiscal decentralization and mobilization of own sources of revenue, which comprises of taxes and non-tax items. Here, we examine transfer of taxes and non-tax items after decentralization, powers given to LGs to levy, collect and effect periodical revision of taxes and non-taxes, problems faced by LGs with regard to revision of tax rates and collection of revenue.

Among the various items of revenue, own source revenue is the most important source of revenue for LGs due to a variety of reasons: (a) there are no conditions attached to own source revenues and the LGs have full freedom to spend according to their priority of expenditure; (b) own source revenue enables the government to bunch each expenditure along with a tax to finance it; (c) own source revenue would ensure that allocative efficiency is maintained by ensuring that the LG equates cost and benefit at the margin. Allocation of own sources of revenue, transfer of items to LGs, assigning powers to levy, collect and revise rates of it are important elements of a sound fiscal decentralization system.

Since the implementation of decentralization, the state government has assigned a few taxes and non-tax items to the LGs as per the new enactment. The KPRA, 1994 (as amended from time to time), empowers the GPs to levy taxes such as property tax, profession tax, advertisement tax, entertainment tax, show tax and service tax. The KMA, 1994 (as amended from time to time), empowers the municipalities and MCs to levy property tax, profession tax, entertainment tax, tax on animals and vessels, show tax, advertisement tax and timber tax. Both the GPs and the aforementioned urban LGs can also levy a surcharge on property tax and service tax/cess on sanitation, water supply, street light and drainage. Besides the taxes, they can levy and collect non-tax revenues like trade license fee, building permit fee, registration fee, fines, rent, etc. On the other hand, other categories of rural LGs such as BPs and DPs do not have the power to collect taxes. They can only collect user charges and receive donations and contributions.

PARTIAL FISCAL DECENTRALIZATION

Though LGs were assigned tax and non-tax items, no new items were transferred; they were not given full powers to revise rates or effect periodical revision. The assignment of taxes and non-tax items has three limitations. First, the state government has not transferred any new tax or non-tax items to LGs since the implementation of decentralized governance. In spite of assignment of a number of additional functions and expenditure responsibilities, no new tax or non-tax item was transferred to LGs. This indicates that there has been an increase in expenditure responsibilities without corresponding assignment of new own source revenue items. Second, the LGs were not given powers to revise rate of taxes and non-tax items. The power to revise the rate of revision was retained by the state government. Third, the LGs were not given powers to revise the rate periodically. Though the KPRA, 1994, and KMA, 1994, stipulate that the property tax is to be revised once in five years, the LGs were not given powers to revise. Thus, fiscal decentralization effected in Kerala with regard to own source revenue and resources is a limited or partial one. In the following section, we examine major items of tax and non-tax levied and collected by LGs in Kerala.

TAX REVENUE

Property Tax

The KPRA, 1994, and KMA, 1994, empower GPs, municipalities and MCs to levy property tax on every building including the apartment thereto situated within the area of the respective LGs. But the LGs were not given powers to revise rate of taxes or effect periodical revision of the tax. These powers were vested with the state government. The rules framed under the aforementioned Acts laid down procedures to levy and collect property tax. Property tax was originally assessed on annual rental value basis in GPs from 1 April 1996 and municipalities and MCs from 1 April 1993. But attempts were made to switch over from annual rental value basis to plinth area basis in 2011. But the actual change was effected by the state government from 1 April 2013. Consequent to this, all GPs switched over to the new system and enhanced the rate of taxation after a long gap of 17 years. However, the municipalities and MCs began to only take steps to switch over to the new system since April 2013. The municipalities told us that it would take at least a year to complete the preparation for switching over to plinth area-based collection of property tax. And the MCs wanted more than one and a half years to complete the work.

Meanwhile, the state government issued a revised order practically withdrawing the revision of property tax of GPs, municipalities and MCs. As per the revised order on 27 March 2015, the following changes were effected: (a) all houses with a plinth area up to 660 sq. feet were exempted from property tax; (b) revised rate was not applicable in the case of existing houses with a plinth area up to 2,000 sq. feet; (c) the total hike should not exceed 25 per cent of the previous tax amount in the case of existing houses with plinth area above 2,000 sq. feet and (d) excess property tax collected on the basis of revised rate has to be adjusted in the subsequent years. Due to this measure, the municipalities and MCs stopped implementation of revision of property tax. The GPs which implemented the revision were forced to repay the amount of taxes collected based on the revised order.

Another disturbing aspect has been the attitude of successive state governments regarding revision of the tax during the last two decades. According to KPRA, 1994, and KMA, 1994, revision of property tax has to be effected once in five years. But the state government has not initiated steps for revision for two decades due to non-formulation of rules. Due to this, the LGs were prevented from implementing periodic revision of property tax, the most important tax of LGs and improving their finances. Thus, lack of powers to revise the rate of taxes and effect periodical revision of tax is the root problem faced by the LGs in Kerala.

The 5th SFC which examined this issue recommended three things: (a) revoke the revised property tax revision order issued by the state government on 27 March 2015, enabling LGs to collect the tax at the pre-revised rate; (b) revise the tax at the expiry of every five years as envisaged in the KPRA, 1994, and the KMA, 1994, and frame necessary rules in this regard; (c) compensate the loss of revenue of the LGs by the state government due to lack of timely revision of property tax as stipulated in KPRA, 1994, and KMA, 1994.

Profession Tax

Profession tax is the second major item of tax collected by GPs, municipalities and MCs. According to KPRA, 1994, and KMA, 1994, profession tax is levied and collected at half yearly on every company which transacts business in the area of LG for not less than 60 days in the aggregate in that half year and every person who is engaged on a profession, art or calling, or transacts business or holds any appointment within the area of such LG for not less than 60 days in that half year. In India, profession tax is collected by the state government in all states except Kerala and Tamil Nadu. A serious problem faced by the LGs in Kerala is the non-revision of the ceiling of the tax for the last 30 years.

As per the Indian Constitution, Parliament is the authority to change the ceiling of the profession tax. The ceiling of the profession tax was ₹250 per year per person at the time of the adoption of the Constitution of India in 1949. It was revised to ₹2,500 per year per person in 1988, after a period of 39 years. Though the successive UFCs had recommended a revision of the ceiling of the tax, no action has been taken to revise the tax since 1988. This indicates that the ceiling limit of the tax has not been revised for three decades.

The 14th UFC had examined this issue and recommended to raise the ceiling from ₹2,500 to ₹12,000 per annum. The Commission recommended that Parliament be empowered to fix this ceiling without going in for a constitutional amendment each time. The Commission also recommended that Article 276 (2) of the Constitution be amended to increase the limits on the imposition of profession tax by states and to empower Parliament to raise the ceiling on profession tax. But no action has been taken towards this direction till now. This long delay in the revision of ceiling of the tax has resulted in enormous loss in revenue of the LGs and affected their finances very badly. Lack of powers of LGs to effect the revision is the root cause of the present situation. This can be cited as a classic case of distorted fiscal decentralization.

A second issue is poor collection of tax due to incomplete data on taxpayers, the attitude of many categories of professionals not to pay the tax, low priority given to collect the tax by LGs, administrative and legal problems in initiating revenue recovery proceedings, inadequate staff in LGs, etc. Due to these reasons, only a portion of the tax potential is tapped by the LGs.

The 5th SFC which examined the issue found that except government employees, majority of professionals like advocates, medical practitioners, tax practitioners, contractors, commission agents, brokers, etc., are not assessed for profession tax due to lack of proper records or incomplete database. The Commission found that most of the employees and workers in the unorganized sector and self-employed persons such as private bus staff, lorry and truck drivers, cleaners, taxi drivers, auto-rickshaw drivers, construction workers, etc., are not assessed for profession tax.

Entertainment Tax

Entertainment tax is the third major item of tax of the GPs, municipalities and MCs. The tax is collected as per the Kerala Local Authorities Entertainments Tax Act, 1961. The tax is levied on events such as exhibition, performance, amusement, game, sport or race for which persons are admitted on payment. Entertainment tax from cinema halls was a major source of revenue of GPs, municipalities and MCs in the past. But due to the unprecedented technological development of entertainment media, a large number of cinema halls were closed. The telecast of cinema in TV channels, introduction of cable and dish televisions, availability of unlimited Internet services at cheap rate, rapid expansion of information technology (IT), enabling viewing of cinemas in mobile phones, computer, laptop, tabs, etc., have reduced the role of cinema theatres. These developments have reduced the tax revenue from the entertainment tax substantially.

Another development was the introduction of Goods and Services Tax (GST) by the central government and the inclusion of entertainment tax in GST from July 2017. With this measure, the LGs lost their power to collect the entertainment tax. And the state government says that the loss in revenue due to this to the LGs will be compensated through appropriate measures but norms on compensation have not been declared by the government so far.

Advertisement Tax

Advertisement tax is the fourth major tax of the GPs, municipalities and MCs. The KPRA, 1994, and KMA, 1994, empower LGs to levy and collect the tax. The tax is levied on a person who erects, exhibits, fixes or retains upon or over any land, building, wall, hoarding or structure, any advertisement or displays in public view in an area coming under GPs, municipalities and MCs. Besides this, advertisement displayed in a public service vehicle is also taxed.

This is not a simple tax. Complex and impracticable procedures are stipulated in KPRA, 1994, and KMA, 1994, for approval of rates, levy and collection of the tax. According to the Acts, an LG who wishes to levy the tax should prepare a bye-law specifying the terms and conditions of levy in the first instance. After preparation, the bye-law should be sent to the director of panchayats/urban affairs for scrutiny and forwarded to Local Self Government Department (LSGD) for notification. Usually, it will take considerable time for issuing notification by the LSGD. Here, the basic issue is the lack of powers of LGs to revise taxes based on simple procedures.

Due to this irrational, complex and time-consuming procedures, only 15 per cent of the LGs are levying the tax. Of the 1,034 LGs which have the power to collect the advertisement tax (941 GPs, 87 municipalities and 6 MCs), only 150 could make bye-laws so far. Thus, lack of bye-laws is the main obstacle in the collection of the tax.

The 5th SFC had examined the issue and recommended radical restructuring in the procedures to levy and collect the tax. It recommended necessary amendments in KPRA, 1994, and KMA, 1994, to do away with the system of bye-laws for levying the tax. Instead, the government should frame advertisement tax rules applicable to all GPs, municipalities and MCs for levy and collection of tax.

Show Tax

Show tax is another tax levied by GPs, municipalities and MCs. It is levied on any entertainment, exhibition, performance, amusement, game, sports or race to which persons are admitted on payment of money. The state government is the authority to fix the minimum rate and other rate of the tax. In GPs, the rate of show tax is fixed as per the Kerala Panchayat Raj (Levy and Collection of Show Tax) Rules, 1995. In municipalities and MCs, the rate of show tax is fixed as per KMA, 1994. The minimum rate of show tax was fixed in municipalities and MCs in 1999 and GPs in 2003. The amount of minimum tax ranged between ₹5 and ₹50. Efforts were not taken to revise the tax since then.

Service Tax/Cess

The KPRA, 1994, and KMA, 1994, empower the GPs, municipalities and MCs to levy service tax/cess on sanitation, water supply, street lighting and drainage wherever such services are provided at the rate fixed by the LGs subject to a minimum rate. The Acts and the rules prescribed the minimum rate to be levied as follows: sanitation

4 per cent, drinking water 3 per cent, street lighting 2 per cent and drainage 1 per cent of the property tax. This service tax is to be collected half yearly along with the property tax.

Though all the GPs, municipalities and MCs have the option to levy the service tax, only a small number of LGs levy the tax. The tax is levied mostly by municipalities and MCs. The wording in the Acts and the rules do not have clarity relating to compulsory collection of the tax. While the KPRA, 1994, clearly states that the GPs shall levy service charges, the KMA, 1994, says that the municipalities may levy service cess. In the rules, the LGs are given an option to collect or not to collect the tax. As per Kerala Panchayat Raj (Property Tax, Service Tax and Surcharge) Rules, 2011, and the Kerala Municipality (Property Tax, Service Cess and Surcharge) Rules, 2011, the LGs may levy service tax/cess as per the rate which should not be less than the minimum rate fixed by the Government. Due to this, most of the GPs opted not to levy the tax. The 5th SFC examined this issue and recommended for compulsory levy. It recommended that KMA, 1994, and rule of 2011 on property tax, service tax and similar rule of panchayats 2011 shall be amended to make levy of service tax/cess by GPs, municipalities and MCs mandatory.

Service Charge on Central Government Buildings

The central government buildings are exempted from the levy of property tax. But the state government can impose a service tax on the buildings owned by the central government. The Kerala Panchayat Raj (Property Tax, Service Tax and Surcharge) Rules, 2011, and Kerala municipality rules for the same authorize the LGs to levy a service charge on central government buildings equivalent to an amount ranging between 33.3 per cent and 75 per cent of the property tax. If all the public services like sanitation, water supply, street lighting, drainage, etc., are provided by the LG, it can levy an amount equivalent to 75 per cent of the property tax as service charge. Though there is provision to levy service charge on central government buildings, the LGs are not levying it. It is pointed out that many of the LGs are unaware of this statutory provisions.

NON-TAX REVENUE

The GPs, municipalities and MCs can collect non-tax revenue like fee for licenses, permits, certificates, etc. The LGs can impose fines and penalties for delayed payment and breach of law relating to the subjects coming under their jurisdiction. All categories of LGs including DPs and BPs can also collect service charges for the service provided by them to the public. The items of non-tax revenue collected by GPs, municipalities and MCs are trade license fee [Dangerous and Offensive [D&O]), building permit fee, registration fee, fee for certificates, cinematograph license fee, market fee, fines and penalties, rent on buildings, income from river sand, etc. Among them, the major items are building permit fee, D&O license fee, fines and penalties and rent on buildings. Though the LGs can collect non-tax revenue, they are not given powers to revise rates and effect periodical revision.

D&O License Fee

This license fee is collected by GPs, municipalities and MCs. As per the Kerala Panchayat Raj (Issue of License to Dangerous and Offensive Trades and Factories) Rules, 1996, which came into force in March, 2003, GPs collect this fee. The fee rate is based on the volume of daily turnover of trade and schedules containing item of commodities traded. The commodities are classified in to four schedules and the first schedule contains 159 items. Lack of periodical revision of the rate of license fee is an issue which needs attention of the government. The state government has not taken steps to enhance the rate of the fee since 2003.

Similar is the situation of the D&O license fee of municipalities and MCs. Though the Kerala Municipality (Issues of License to D&O Trades, Other Trades and Factories) Rules, 2011, have been notified on 25 January 2011 with a view to increase the rate, it has not been implemented. It is disturbing to note that the state government has not taken any steps to implement the decision and orders were issued seven times to keep the rules in abeyance.

Building Permit Fee

Another item of fee collected by GPs, municipalities and MCs is building permit fee. The Kerala Panchayat Building Rules, 2011, and the Kerala Municipality Building Rules, 1999, have been formulated with the purpose of regulating construction of buildings. A person who wishes to construct a building will have to submit a plan of the building to the concerned GPs, municipalities or MCs for issue of building permit. After examining the plan, location of the buildings, assignment of the area for road construction or other specified purposes mentioned in the town or area plan, a building permit is issued. The LGs collect a fee, namely building permit fee for the purpose. The rate of the building permit fee was fixed in GPs in 2011 and municipalities and MCs in 2010. No steps have been taken to enhance the rate of fee since then, implying that the state government has not taken steps to revise the rate of fee periodically.

Rent on Buildings

Rent from buildings is another source of non-tax revenue of rural as well as urban LGs. LGs own different types of buildings like shopping complexes, commercial buildings, community halls, auditoriums, etc. The 5th SFC which examined the rate of rent charged by LGs found that the rates were very low compared to the open market rate. It was found that in some cases of community halls and auditoriums, the rent charged was not sufficient to cover even the electricity, water and cleaning charges of it. There is no justification for following a policy of charging rates below the cost of operation and maintenance (O&M). There is a need for rationalization and periodic revision of rates. And the state government should fix norms for the purpose.

Other Items of Non-tax Revenues

The LGs are collecting fee to issue licenses and certificates for different purposes. The important certificates issued are those of birth, death, marriage, residence and ownership. Other certificates issued are residential certificate for ration card, unemployment, personal identification, private hospitals, age certificates of building, etc. Similarly, fees are collected for issuing various licenses, permissions, registration of institutions, etc. The fees charged for the certificates, licenses, services, etc., were very low and fixed much earlier. Steps have not been taken to revise the rates periodically. In this context, there is considerable scope for enhancing the rate of fees and effecting periodical revision. The 5th SFC had examined this issue and recommended to raise rate of the aforementioned items of non-tax by at least 50 per cent.

CONCLUSION

The aforementioned analysis can be concluded with the following observations. The fiscal decentralization that was implemented in Kerala is partial or limited. Though the LGs were assigned taxes and non-tax items, no new items were transferred and they were not given powers to revise rate or effect periodical revision. The state government had not transferred any new tax or non-tax items to LGs since the implementation of decentralized governance, in spite of assignment of a number of additional functions and expenditure responsibilities. The LGs were not given powers to revise rate of taxes and non-tax items and effect periodical revision. The power to revise the rate revision was retained by the state government.

Though the state government retained powers to revise rate of taxes and non-tax items, the government had not taken steps to effect periodical revision for about two decades. Efforts were not taken to change provisions of acts, rules and procedures for revision of rates. The state policy of neglecting own resource mobilization of LGs and providing funds through devolution and transfer have increased the dependence of LGs on transferred resources.

Regarding revision of rates of LGs, the successive state governments in Kerala have followed a distorted fiscal decentralization approach. Though KPRA, 1994, and KMA, 1994, authorize the state government to revise the rate of property tax of the LGs once in five years, the successive governments in Kerala have not revised the rate accordingly. A revision of the tax effected after a gap of 17 years was practically withdrawn. The upper ceiling of the profession tax, the second major item of tax of LGs which was fixed in 1988 was not revised due to indifferent attitude of the successive governments at the centre. The inclusion of entertainment tax, the third major item of tax of LGs in the newly introduced GST has resulted in considerable revenue loss to the LGs. Norms to compensate the loss of revenue has not been worked out so far. The retrogressive and outdated bye-law system followed with regard to advertisement tax stands as an obstacle to introduce or revise the rate of tax in the LGs.

Though all the GPs, municipalities and MCs can levy advertisement tax, only 15 per cent of the LGs collect it due to the practical problems associated with the introduction of the tax. Due to the lack of clarity in KPRA, 1994, KMA, 1994, and the rules framed relating to compulsory collection of service tax, majority of the LGs are not collecting the tax. Though the existing laws and rules authorize the LGs to collect a service charge on central government building, the LGs are not collecting it either due to laxity of tax collection or ignorance. The situation is not different with respect to non-tax items. The rate of fees levied for licenses, permits, certificates, etc., are very low, fixed several years ago and not revised periodically.

From the earlier text, it is clear that the successive state governments in Kerala have not taken steps to revise the rate of taxes or fees periodically. Efforts were not made to make appropriate changes in the provisions of Acts or rules for the purpose. The thinking of the successive governments in Kerala was that periodical revision of rate of taxes and fees was an anti-people measure or politically undesirable thing. This unsound policy of the state government has resulted in steady deterioration in mobilization efforts of own resources of municipalities and MCs. The GPs, municipalities and MCs also give very low priority for revision of rates of tax and non-tax revenue and expanding tax base.

Finances of Gram Panchayats

Though Kerala had implemented fiscal decentralization, the actual transfer of fiscal powers is limited. Powers are not given to LGs for revision of rate of taxes and non-tax items, allotment of money on its discretion, freedom to spend money for various purposes, etc. The state government regulates and interferes in fiscal matters of LGs through Acts such as KPRA, 1994, KMA, 1994, a host of rules, auditing of accounts and a number of controls. Powers are not given to effect revenue recovery from defaulters. The staff working in LGs are government staff and their transfer and posting are done by the state government. We have to examine the finances of LGs in this context.

This chapter examines the finances of GPs, based on the fiscal data collected from 56 sample GPs. It examines the growth and structure of receipts as well as expenditure and major issues relating to the finances of GP.

The data for the study were collected from a sample of 56 GPs belonging to all districts of Kerala using a structured schedule. A multi-stage random sampling method was used to select the samples. The GPs were classified into three geographic regions such as coastal, midland and highland or hilly regions. The samples were selected based on it. The sample GPs account for 6 per cent of the total number of GPs in Kerala (Table 4.1). For the analysis, we have used the total receipts and expenditure per GP.

GROWTH AND STRUCTURE OF RECEIPTS

The items of receipts of GPs may be classified into five items, namely (a) tax and non-tax revenue, (b) transfer of funds from the state

Table 4.1 *Distribution of Sample GPs*

Sl No.	Name of District	Total Number of GPs	Number of Sample GPs	Sample Size (%)
1	Thiruvananthapuram	73	4	5.48
2	Kollam	68	4	5.88
3	Pathanamthitta	53	4	7.55
4	Alappuzha	72	4	5.56
5	Kottayam	71	4	5.63
6	Idukki	52	4	7.69
7	Ernakulam	82	3	3.66
8	Thrissur	86	4	4.65
9	Palakkad	88	4	4.55
10	Malappuram	94	5	5.32
11	Kozhikode	70	4	5.71
12	Wayanad	23	4	17.39
13	Kannur	71	4	5.63
14	Kasargod	38	4	10.53
	Total	**941**	**56**	**5.95**

resources, (c) the World Bank loan and 13th UFC grants, (d) centrally sponsored schemes (CSS) and welfare pension receipts and (e) borrowings. Major items of tax collected by GPs are property tax, profession tax, entertainment tax, advertisement tax, show tax and service tax. Important items of non-tax revenue collected by GPs are trade license fee (D&O), building permit fee, rents on buildings and fee for issuing licenses and certificates. In Chapter 3, we had a detailed discussion on the taxes and non-tax revenue collected, problems faced and major issues of these.

The average total receipts received per GP ranged from ₹486.15 lakhs to ₹806.27 lakhs between 2011–2012 and 2014–2015. Table 4.2 gives the growth and structure of the receipts of GPs for a period of four years from 2011–2012 to 2014–2015. A review of the trend in total receipts indicates considerable yearly fluctuations. This was

Table 4.2 *Total Receipts per GP: Amount, Composition and Growth Rate*

Item	2011–2012	2012–2013	2013–2014	2014–2015
(₹ in Thousands)				
Tax	2,890.62	3,463.52	3,721.72	5,295.21
Non-tax	2,434.99	2,296.40	1,634.70	1,691.07
Total transfer of funds	185,74.80	20,996.21	28,060.76	29,688.89
World Bank loan	1,162.55	1,813.03	1,841.02	1,981.79
13th UFC grants	2,684.71	3,771.28	4,128.16	6,090.53
CSS	12,603.44	17,289.40	16,818.86	19,176.80
Welfare pensions	7,184.30	10,597.12	11,326.06	16,181.32
Borrowing	1,080.18	285.79	248.38	522.14
Total	**48,615.59**	**60,512.75**	**67,779.64**	**80,627.75**
Composition (%)				
Tax	5.9	5.7	5.5	6.6
Non-tax	5.0	3.8	2.4	2.1
Total transfer of funds	38.2	34.7	41.4	36.8
World Bank loan	2.4	3.0	2.7	2.5
13th UFC grants	5.5	6.2	6.1	7.6
CSS	25.9	28.6	24.8	23.8
Welfare pensions	14.8	17.5	16.7	20.1
Borrowing	2.2	0.5	0.4	0.6
Total	**100.0**	**100.0**	**100.0**	**100.0**
Growth Rate (%)				
Tax		19.8	7.5	42.3
Non-tax		–5.7	–28.8	3.4
Total transfer of funds		13.0	33.6	5.8
World Bank loan		56.0	1.5	7.6
13th UFC grants		40.5	9.5	47.5
CSS		37.2	–2.7	14.0
Welfare pensions		47.5	6.9	42.9
Borrowing		–73.5	–13.1	110.2
Total		**24.5**	**12.0**	**19.0**

due to the carry-over of unspent amount of a year to subsequent years and delayed receipts of CSS and welfare pensions.

An analysis of the structure of receipts gives the following broad changes. The share of tax and non-tax revenue ranged between 9 and 11 per cent during the period. The transfer of funds from the SOTR comprising General Purpose Fund (GPF), maintenance fund and development fund ranged between 37 and 38 per cent. The World Bank loan and grants from 13th UFC accounts for 8 to 10 per cent. The funds received from the CSS from the Union Government accounts for nearly one-fourth of the total receipts. The social welfare pensions of the state government, distributed through the GPs, accounts for 15 to 20 per cent of the total receipts. The amount of funds received through borrowing was very small and not even accounted for 1 per cent of the total receipts of the GPs except in one year. Thus, the structure of revenue of GPs shows that the share of tax and non-tax revenue is very small or less than 10 per cent. A notable aspect about the finances of GPs is its heavy reliance on funds transferred from the state and other grants for meeting its activities connected with administration, provision of civic and mandatory services, maintenance of own assets and assets of TIs and annual plans. Thus, the availability of meagre own resources and lack of authority to increase rate of taxes and non-tax items assigned to LGs are the weak points in the finances of GPs.

Tax and Non-tax Revenue

We may start the analysis with an examination of the amount of tax revenue collected by GPs. The average amount of revenue collected from various taxes per GP for a period of four years is given in Table 4.3. Property tax is the tax which accounted for major share of tax collected. Profession tax is the second major item of tax and its share was 31 per cent in 2014–2015. The share of revenue from entertainment, advertisement and other items was very small. The change in method of assessment of property tax from annual rental value basis to plinth area basis, implemented during 2014–2015, had increased collection of the tax by 71 per cent. But the subsequent reduction in the rate of tax and exemption given to certain categories had resulted

Table 4.3 Tax Revenue per GP: Amount, Growth Rate and Composition

Item	2011–2012 (₹ in Thousand)	2012–2013 (₹ in Thousand)	2013–2014 (₹ in Thousand)	2014–2015 (₹ in Thousand)	2014–2015 Composition (%)
Profession tax	1,247.98	1,472.82	1,494.96	1,621.86	30.6
Property tax	1,508.54	1,792.58	2,053.17	3,508.84	66.3
Entertainment	45.74	76.01	68.98	67.32	1.3
Advertisement	4.86	5.57	6.02	9.19	0.2
Other taxes	83.50	116.55	98.59	88.01	1.7
Total	2,890.62	3,463.52	3,721.72	5,295.21	100
Growth rate (%)	–	19.8	7.5	42.3	–

in steep fall in the growth of revenue in the subsequent years. The taxes which registered a fall in revenue during the four-year period were entertainment and other items of taxes. A review of the trends in growth of taxes collected shows that the only factor which contributed to a substantial increase in collection of the tax during 2014–2015 was due to the change in assessment of the property tax.

An analysis of the trends in non-tax revenue gives a dismal picture (Table 4.4). Based on the data shown in Table 4.4, we can make the following inferences. There had been a negative growth in total non-tax revenue collected for two years. The growth of the revenue in 2014–2015 was marginal. In the case of building permit fee, sale of sand and other non-tax items, there had been a fall in revenue. On the other hand, the items of revenue which witnessed a growth were rent on buildings, D&O license and fines/penalties.

Regarding collection of tax arrears, the situation is not different. The amount and composition of tax arrears are given in Table 4.5. Property tax accounted for 55 per cent of the total arrears of tax in 2011–2012. River sand, rent on buildings and profession tax were the other major items that accounted for another 40 per cent. But there had been a substantial change in the composition of arrears in 2014–2015. Of the total arrears, property tax alone accounted for 92 per cent. This indicates the need for strengthening the tax collection machinery and improving efficiency of collection of the property tax.

Devolution of Funds

Prior to the enactment of KPRA, 1994, and KMA, 1994, Kerala had been transferring funds to the GPs in the form of assigned taxes, shared taxes and certain kind of grants for general purposes and for specific purposes both under plan and non-plan. Consequent to the transfer of functions and functionaries as per the aforementioned Acts, more state resources were transferred to LGs based on the recommendation of the newly constituted SFCs. The 1st SFC listed 23 items of grants to LGs that were being paid. Besides the assigned and shared taxes, the 1st SFC recommended a share of 1 per cent of taxes for non-plan non-statutory purpose for traditional functions. Thus, the concept of

Table 4.4 Non-tax Revenue per GP: Amount, Growth Rate and Composition

Item	2011–2012 (₹ in Thousand)	2012–2013 (₹ in Thousand)	2013–2014 (₹ in Thousand)	2014–15 (₹ in Thousand)	2014–2015 Composition (%)
Building permit fee	123.39	225.13	78.47	145.05	8.58
Rent on buildings	267.23	256.67	308.31	332.24	19.65
D&O licence	78.99	87.78	116.17	115.50	6.82
Fines/Penalties	85.46	106.36	132.96	113.35	6.70
Sale of sand	620.24	611.74	304.63	259.18	15.33
Market fee for public market	19.89	21.30	14.44	29.26	1.73
Other non-taxes	1,239.80	987.43	679.72	696.49	41.19
Total	**2,434.99**	**2,296.40**	**1,634.70**	**1,691.07**	**100**
Growth rate (%)	–	–5.7	–28.8	3.4	

Table 4.5 *Tax Arrears per GP in 2011–2012 and 2014–2015*

	2011–2012		2014–2015	
Item	Amount (₹ in Thousand)	Composition (%)	Amount (₹ in Thousand)	Composition (%)
Property tax	595.39	55.1	1,617.53	91.8
River sand	243.50	22.5	0.00	0.0
Rent on buildings	115.67	10.7	27.66	1.6
Profession tax	83.71	7.7	56.98	3.2
Service tax	15.82	1.5	27.59	1.6
Others	26.46	2.4	32.67	1.9
Total	**1,080.53**	**100**	**1,762.43**	**100**

General Purpose Grant, encompassing state support for traditional activities, had evolved through the recommendation of SFC.

The 2nd SFC made a radical change in the approach on assigning and sharing specific taxes. It recommended a shift away from the system of assigning and sharing specific taxes and awarding a host of grants to a system of sharing taxes in toto as General Purpose Grant. For annual development plans, a system of sharing of a certain percentage of state plan resources was introduced.

The approach followed by the 3rd SFC was much different from the earlier ones. In a major change, the 3rd SFC recommended that all transfers including fund for annual development plans should be devolved as a percentage of SOTR. The Commission recommended the devolution based on $(t-3)$ method indicating a devolution based on the actual SOTR collected three years back. Here, t is the year of devolution and $t-3$ is the year prior to three years. In other words, SOTR collected in 2008–2009 will be taken as base for devolution in 2011–2012.

The 4th SFC, which devolved state resources for the five-year period from 2011–2012 to 2015–2016, made further changes in the devolution approach. The Commission recommended the following: (a) devolution of 3.5 per cent of SOTR as GPF using the $t-2$ method, that is, for devolution of year (t), the tax collection of $t-2$ or two years back will be taken; (b) maintenance fund for road and non-road at the rate of 4.5 per cent of SOTR for 2011–2012, 5 per cent for 2012–2013 and 5.5 per cent for the remaining three years based on $t-2$ method; (c) the fund recommended for annual development plan of LG was a share of the assumed plan size of the state (25% in 2011–2012, 27.5% in 2012–2013, 28.5% in 2013–2014, 29.5% in 2014–2015 and 30% in 2015–2016). The amount of funds allotted to annual plan includes the World Bank loans and grants received from the Union Government as per the recommendations of 13th UFC.

Based on 4th SFC recommendations, three items of funds were transferred to the LGs during the period. In case of GPF and maintenance fund, the actual transfer was based on the recommendations of the 4th SFC. But the actual transfer of development fund was lower than the amount recommended by the 4th SFC. During the award period of five years between 2011–2012 and 2015–2016, development fund transferred to LGs was lower compared to the amount recommended by 4th SFC in all years except 2014–2015 (State Finance Commission 2015, Part I, Chapter 10). In this context, we examine the actual amount received by the GPs through the recommendations of the 4th SFC.

Table 4.6 gives the amount received per GP through devolution during first four years of the 4th SFC award period. The total amount received ranged between ₹224.22 lakh and ₹377.61 lakh during the four years. An analysis of composition of devolved funds indicates the following pattern of changes. The share of GPF meant for meeting expenditure of mandatory functions, other basic functions and covering deficits in own funds accounted for 17.9 to 18.6 per cent of total devolved funds.

Maintenance fund given for road maintenance of the GPs ranged between 12.2 and 14.5 per cent. The fund used for maintenance of roads comes under the jurisdiction of GPs. According to existing guidelines, the fund can be utilized for repair, patch work, special repair works, resurfacing of roads, construction of drainage system, repair of culverts, bridges, etc. The guideline permits to utilize the surplus of the fund for construction of new roads and upgradation of

Table 4.6 *Amount Received per GP through Devolution, Central Grants, etc.: Amount, Growth Rate and Composition*

Item	2011–2012 (₹ in Thousand)	2012–2013 (₹ in Thousand)	2013–2014 (₹ in Thousand)	2014–2015 (₹ in Thousand)	2014–2015 Composition (%)
General Purpose Fund	4,007.03	4,910.98	5,904.83	7,041.41	18.6
Development fund (excluding World Bank assistance and 13th FC grant)	10,703.17	11,256.61	14,645.38	15,082.01	39.9
Maintenance fund (road)	2,724.54	3,277.31	4,925.49	5,067.61	13.4
Maintenance fund (non-road)	1,140.05	1,551.31	2,585.05	2,497.85	6.6
Subtotal	**18,574.80**	**20,996.21**	**28,060.76**	**29,688.89**	**78.6**
World Bank loan	1,162.55	1,813.03	1,841.02	1,981.79	5.2
13th UFC grant	2,684.71	3,771.28	4,128.16	6,090.53	16.1
Subtotal	**3,847.26**	**5,584.31**	**5,969.18**	**8,072.32**	**21.4**
Grand total	**22,422.05**	**26,580.51**	**34,029.94**	**37,761.21**	**100.0**

	Growth (%)		
General Purpose Fund	22.6	20.2	19.2
Development fund (excluding World Bank assistance and 13th FC grant)	5.2	30.1	3.0
Maintenance fund (road)	20.3	50.3	2.9
Maintenance fund (non-road)	36.1	66.6	–3.4
Subtotal	13.0	33.6	5.8
World Bank assistance	56.0	1.5	7.6
13th CFC grant	40.5	9.5	47.5
Subtotal	45.2	6.9	35.2
Grand total	18.5	28.0	11.0

roads. Similarly, maintenance fund given for non-road items can be utilized for repair and maintenance of own buildings of GPs and TIs like hospitals, schools, etc. The fund may be also used for payment of electricity charges, water charges, purchase of furniture for schools, purchase of medicines, hospital equipment, computers, computer accessories, consumables, medicines, machineries, etc. Maintenance fund given for non-road assets ranged between 5.1 and 7.6 per cent.

Development fund is the third item of the transferred fund. It is a fund meant to finance annual development plans of GPs for the local-level development. The GPs have freedom to formulate and execute annual plan consisting of a number of projects and schemes for local development, subject to the overall plan guidelines of the state government. The fund consists of a share of the state plan funded from state resources and borrowing, the World Bank loan and 13th UFC grant. Of the total transferred funds, development fund comprising the earlier items accounted for 60 to 65 per cent. Table 4.6 gives the item-wise components of development fund.

A review of the trends in growth rate of devolved funds indicates a steep fall in the year 2014–2015. The items which witnessed a decline are development fund excluding the World Bank assistance and 13th UFC grant and maintenance fund for road and non-road.

Centrally Sponsored Schemes and Social Welfare Schemes

The GPs execute agency functions such as implementation of CSS of the Union Government and welfare pension schemes of the state government. Under the CSS, the major items are flood relief, Integrated Child Development Services (ICDS), Mahatma Gandhi National Rural Employment Guarantee Scheme (MGNREGS) and total sanitation. The other schemes are Indira Awas Yojana (IAY), Kudumbashree, MP Fund, Sarva Shiksha Abhiyan (SSA), Swarnajayanti Gram Swarozgar Yojana (SGSY), Swarna Jayanti Shahari Rozgar Yojana (SJSRY), etc. Table 4.7 gives the CSS receipts per GP for a period of four years from 2011–2012 to 2014–2015. A review of the growth in the CSS receipts

Table 4.7 CSS Receipts per GP: Amount, Growth Rate and Composition

Item	2011–2012 (₹ in Thousand)	2012–2013 (₹ in Thousand)	2013–2014 (₹ in Thousand)	2014–2015 (₹ in Thousand)	2014–2015 Composition (%)
Flood relief	128.49	293.65	309.63	395.91	2.06
IAY	21.11	15.93	0.96	0.58	0.00
ICDS	318.66	322.25	349.80	348.66	1.82
Kudumbashree	48.06	16.77	5.26	11.40	0.06
MP Fund	53.23	152.45	125.08	94.57	0.49
MGNREGS	9,898.17	14,941.23	13,670.63	16,415.28	85.60
SSA	98.57	49.96	42.25	27.01	0.14
Total sanitation	79.04	202.05	313.31	284.84	1.49
SGSY/SJSRY	746.32	47.89	90.15	0	0.00
Others	1,211.79	1,247.23	1,911.80	1,598.55	8.34
Total	12,603.44	17,289.40	16,818.86	19,176.80	100
Growth rate (%)		37.2	–2.7	14.0	

indicates a negative growth in 2013–2014. Among the schemes, the single largest scheme was MGNREGS.

The main goal of MGNREGS is to provide a strong safety net for the vulnerable groups by providing a fallback employment source, when other employment alternatives are scarce or inadequate. Mahatma Gandhi National Rural Employment Guarantee Act (MGNREGA) is a powerful instrument for inclusive growth in rural India through its impact on social protection, livelihood security and democratic empowerment. The primary objective of the Act is augmenting wage employment for the poorest of the poor while the secondary objective is to strengthen natural resources management through works that address causes of chronic poverty arising due to drought and, thus, encourage sustainable development. The scheme aims to provide at least 100 days of guaranteed wage employment in a financial year to every person below poverty line (BPL) and above poverty line (APL) households whose adult members volunteer to do unskilled manual work.

The state government had transferred the functions of delivery of social welfare pensions to the GPs. Here, the funds are given by the state government and the role of GPs is to distribute the pensions periodically to actual beneficiaries directly or through postal transfer or through bank accounts. The important schemes are agricultural workers pension, destitute/widow pension, disabled pension, old-age pension and unemployment allowance given to unemployed educated youth. Table 4.8 presents the amount of welfare pension receipts of GPs for a period of four years. The total amount distributed ranged between ₹71.84 lakh and ₹161.81 lakh during the period. A serious problem faced by the GPs has been inadequate staff to meet the implementation of the schemes. Though a number of CSS schemes and social welfare pensions were transferred to GPs, adequate additional staff was not given to GPs.

GROWTH AND STRUCTURE OF EXPENDITURE

The expenditure is classified into eight items, namely administration, establishment, annual plan, maintenance, O&M, miscellaneous,

Table 4.8 Welfare Pension Receipts per GP: Amount, Growth Rate and Composition

Item	2011–2012 (₹ in Thousand)	2012–2013 (₹ in Thousand)	2013–2014 (₹ in Thousand)	2014–2015 (₹ in Thousand)	2014–2015 Composition (%)
Agricultural workers pension	2,175.27	2,121.00	2,036.05	2,854.61	17.64
Financial help for widow's daughters marriage	64.78	79.22	130.71	170.46	1.05
IGN destitute/widow pension	2,269.72	4,176.54	5,023.17	5,998.17	37.07
IGN disabled pension	909.92	1,534.98	1,953.37	2,362.72	14.60
IGN old-age pension	828.24	1,745.27	1,035.01	3,663.38	22.64
Pension for unmarried women aged above 50	136.31	207.35	270.24	380.34	2.35
Production incentive to paddy growers	98.70	65.09	103.16	158.92	0.98
Unemployment allowance	282.83	280.89	130.87	265.69	1.64
Others	418.52	386.77	643.47	327.03	2.03
Total	**7,184.30**	**10,597.12**	**11,326.06**	**16,181.32**	**100**
Growth rate (%)		**47.50**	**39.08**	**42.87**	

CSS and welfare pension. The average total expenditure per GP ranged between ₹480.76 lakh and ₹727.64 lakh during the period 2011–2012 and 2014–2015 (Table 4.9). An examination of structure of expenditure indicates the following. Annual plan accounts for the single largest share of expenditure. It ranged between 34 and 44 per cent of the total expenditure. Welfare pension is the second major item of expenditure ranging between 14 and 24 per cent of the total expenditure. Expenditure on CSS, establishment and maintenance rank third, fourth and fifth positions, respectively. The other items of expenditure are O&M, miscellaneous and administration. Thus, an important aspect of the structure of expenditure has been the spending of about 40 per cent of the total expenditure on social welfare pensions and CSS.

A review of the growth in total expenditure indicates the following trend. The year 2012–2013 witnessed a high growth followed by a decline in the subsequent years. This may be due to spending of balance amount of a financial year in the subsequent year and delayed receipts of CSS and welfare pensions. In the case of certain items, there exist wide fluctuations in growth. During the year 2014–2015, four items, namely CSS, annual plan, maintenance and O&M registered a negative growth in expenditure.

Administration and Establishment

An attempt is made to examine major individual items of expenditure consisting of office expenses of GP, expenses related to TIs, expenses connected with organization and conduct of the meeting of gram sabha, electricity charges of office buildings, rents paid for the buildings hired and other items. Table 4.10 presents administrative expenses per GP for a period of four years. The total administrative expenditure per GP ranged between ₹9.16 lakh and ₹11.23 lakh during the period. Office expenses accounted for largest item followed by expenses of TIs and electricity charges.

Establishment expenditure is another item related to the payments given to staff, president, elected members of GP, etc. The items coming under this category are salary, wages, travelling allowances (TAs), pension contribution of staff, honorarium and TA paid to president

Table 4.9 *Total Expenditure per GP: Amount, Composition and Growth*

Item of Expenditure	2011–2012	2012–2013	2013–2014	2014–2015
($ in Thousands)				
Administrative	916.17	857.60	971.24	1,123.76
CSS	12,722.58	13,848.44	13,280.94	13,001.63
Annual plan	17,765.37	27,286.63	27,548.67	24,750.81
Establishment	4,549.66	4,819.15	5,775.69	6,562.89
Maintenance	2,882.37	2,385.96	7,761.99	6,490.58
Miscellaneous	802.03	676.43	1,396.40	1,564.55
O&M	1,653.19	1,729.60	1,823.26	1,810.17
Welfare pension	6,785.07	10,551.94	10,779.85	17,460.45
Total	**48,076.44**	**62,155.74**	**69,338.04**	**72,764.85**
Composition (%)				
Administrative	1.91	1.38	1.40	1.54
CSS	26.46	22.28	19.15	17.87
Annual plan	36.95	43.90	39.73	34.01
Establishment	9.46	7.75	8.33	9.02
Maintenance	6.00	3.84	11.19	8.92
Miscellaneous	1.67	1.09	2.01	2.15
O&M	3.44	2.78	2.63	2.49
Welfare pension	14.11	16.98	15.55	24.00
Total	**100.00**	**100.00**	**100.00**	**100.00**
Growth (%)				
Administrative		−6.4	13.3	15.7
CSS		8.8	−4.1	−2.1
Annual plan		53.6	1.0	−10.2
Establishment		5.9	19.8	13.6
Maintenance		−17.2	225.3	−16.4
Miscellaneous		−15.7	106.4	12.0
O&M		4.6	5.4	−0.7
Welfare pension		55.5	2.2	62.0
Total		**29.3**	**11.6**	**4.9**

Table 4.10 *Administrative Expenditure per GP: Amount, Growth Rate and Composition*

Item	2011–2012 (₹ in Thousand)	2012–2013 (₹ in Thousand)	2013–2014 (₹ in Thousand)	2014–2015 (₹ in Thousand)	2014–2015 Composition (%)
Office expenses	401.43	319.11	387.89	336.60	30.0
Expenses relating to transferred institutions	53.43	81.01	65.88	75.18	6.7
Gram/ ward sabha expenses	17.23	27.95	26.31	19.65	1.7
Office electricity charges	73.68	80.77	78.26	66.21	5.9
Rent on buildings	11.22	11.24	12.45	13.70	1.2
Other items	359.18	337.54	400.46	612.43	54.5
Total	916.17	**857.60**	**971.24**	**1,123.76**	**100**
Growth rate		–6.4	13.3	15.7	

and elected members of GP, etc. Table 4.11 gives establishment expenditure per GP for a period of four years. The total establishment expenditure ranged between ₹45.49 lakh and ₹65.62 lakh for four years. Salaries of permanent staff, wages of temporary staff and pension contribution of staff accounts for about 82 per cent of the total establishment expenditure. Honorarium, sitting fees and TAs of president and members of GP are the other items of establishment expenditure.

Annual Plan Expenditure

GPs allot plan funds to various sectors based on the plan formulation guidelines of the state government. The sector-wise division of the plan expenditure is infrastructure, production, service and others not included in the sector classification. The annual plan expenditure includes the spillover expenditure of the plan projects and schemes

Table 4.11 Establishment Expenditure per GP: Amount, Growth Rate and Composition

Item	2011–2012 (₹ in Thousand)	2012–2013 (₹ in Thousand)	2013–2014 (₹ in Thousand)	2014–2015 (₹ in Thousand)	2014–2015 Composition (%)
Salary	2,950.13	3,256.60	3,895.99	4,463.71	68.01
Wages	267.63	309.95	374.09	591.52	9.01
Honorarium and sitting fees of president, etc.	580.50	598.30	792.13	789.07	12.02
Pension contributions (rural LG only)	284.50	302.76	322.95	311.88	4.75
TA of employees	52.68	75.88	65.27	68.68	1.05
TA of president, vice-president and members (rural LG only)	30.72	35.05	32.00	28.65	0.44
Other expenditure	382.50	240.60	293.27	309.38	4.72
Total	4,549.66	4,819.15	5,775.69	6,562.89	100.00
Growth rate (%)		5.9	19.8	13.6	

of the previous year. The annual plan expenditure per GP ranged between ₹177.65 lakh to ₹275.48 lakh during the period between 2011–2012 and 2014–2015. Table 4.12 gives annual plan expenditure, its composition and growth for a period of four years. An analysis of the composition of expenditure shows that major share of it was spent for service sector schemes during the four years except one year. Plan expenditure for production sector ranged between 15 and 21 per cent during the four-year period. The share of infrastructure sector accounted for 15 to 31 per cent. The share of expenditure on projects not included in infrastructure, production and service sectors ranged between 4 and 6 per cent during the period except one year. From Table 4.12, we can make the following inferences about the trend, composition and problems of plan expenditure. A positive aspect was the steady growth in expenditure on productive sector indicating growth in expenditure for agriculture and allied activities. But a negative aspect was the decline or negative growth in expenditure on infrastructure. Low priority assigned to infrastructure items is a serious issue which needs the urgent attention of GPs. Similarly, the overemphasis and allotment of major share of plan expenditure for service sector was also an unhealthy aspect. Steep decline in expenditure on projects not included in the sector classification was another serious issue. The GPs may face peculiar problems due to geographic location in coastal area, hilly area, water-bound area, islands, etc. Similarly, development requirement of a GP having sizeable tribal population, landless people and elderly people will be different from others. Here, projects other than the traditional sector classifications are required. GPs facing the aforementioned problems due to rigidity in guidelines of the plan formulation do not have freedom to opt for suitable projects. This indicates the need for giving more freedom to GPs to implement projects and schemes taking into consideration the peculiar geographic features and social requirements.

Maintenance Expenditure

As per the recommendations of SFC, maintenance funds are distributed to GPs for maintaining the assets of their own and TIs. The fund is used for two purposes, namely maintenance of road assets and non-road

Table 4.12 Expenditure on Decentralized Plan per GP: Amount, Growth Rate and Composition

Item	2011–2012 (₹ in Thousand)	2012–2013 (₹ in Thousand)	2013–2014 (₹ in Thousand)	2014–2015 (₹ in Thousand)	2014–2015 Composition (%)
Infrastructure sector	5,287.05	6,051.76	4,009.00	3,738.11	15.1
Productive sector	2,688.16	4,104.81	4,899.33	5,209.90	21.0
Projects not included in sector division	3,205.67	1,031.52	1,513.86	1,462.82	5.9
Service sector	6,584.49	16,098.54	17,126.49	14,339.98	57.9
Total	17,765.37	27,286.63	27,548.67	24,750.81	100.0
Growth rate (%)		53.6	1.0	–10.2	

Table 4.13 *Maintenance Expenditure per GP: Amount, Growth Rate and Composition*

Item	2011–2012 (₹ in Thousand)	2012–2013 (₹ in Thousand)	2013–2014 (₹ in Thousand)	2014–2015 (₹ in Thousand)	2014–2015 Composition (%)
Non-road assets	841.85	710.86	2,400.86	1,833.98	28.3
Road assets	2,040.52	1,675.10	5,361.13	4,656.60	71.7
Total	2,882.37	2,385.96	7,761.99	6,490.58	100.0
Growth rate (%)		–17.2	225.3	–16.4	

assets. After meeting maintenance needs, the surplus fund is used for construction of new roads and upgradation of roads. Table 4.13 presents the maintenance expenditure per GP for four years. The GPs spent an annual amount ranging between ₹28.82 lakh and ₹77.61 lakh as maintenance for four years. An analysis of the composition of maintenance fund shows that 69 to 72 per cent of the fund was spent for maintenance of the roads belonging to GPs. In Kerala, there has been huge demand for constructing new roads as well as upgrading the existing roads from the public. One of the significant achievements of decentralization in Kerala has been the construction of rural roads by the GPs.

The expenditure on maintenance of non-road assets like own buildings of GPs and buildings of TIs like schools, hospitals, veterinary centres, krishi bhavans, etc., account for 29 to 31 per cent of the fund. A review of the trends in growth of maintenance expenditure of road and non-road assets shows that there had been a fall in expenditure in 2012–2013. It registered a substantial increase in 2013–2014 and witnessed a fall in the subsequent year.

Operation and Maintenance Expenditure

Besides the maintenance expenditure mentioned earlier, another item is O&M. This includes electricity charges for street lights, water charges for street taps, fuel expenses of vehicles, sanitation expenses and other repair and maintenance expenses. Table 4.14 gives O&M

Table 4.14 O&M Expenditure per GP: Amount, Growth Rate and Composition

Item	2011–2012 (₹ in Thousand)	2012–2013 (₹ in Thousand)	2013–2014 (₹ in Thousand)	2014–2015 (₹ in Thousand)	2014–2015 Composition (%)
Repairs and maintenance expenditure of other assets (not included in plan)	197.85	154.52	296.25	180.39	10.0
Electricity charges for street lights	406.44	521.26	666.14	717.71	39.6
Water charges for street taps	551.88	501.72	381.58	466.02	25.7
Repairs and maintenance expenditure of buildings (not included in plan)	132.17	187.25	24.32	18.75	1.0
Diesel, petrol, gas and lubricants for vehicle	70.59	82.90	109.16	119.14	6.6
Sanitation expenses	77.60	51.30	108.59	98.30	5.4
Other items	216.67	230.65	262.21	209.87	11.6
Total	**1,653.19**	**1,729.60**	**1,823.26**	**1,810.17**	**100**
Growth rate		**4.62**	**5.42**	**-0.72**	

expenditure per GP for a period of four years. The total O&M expenditure range between ₹16.53 lakh and ₹18.10 lakh during the four years. The composition of expenditure shows that nearly 30 per cent of it was spent as electricity charges for street lighting. The amount was paid to Kerala State Electricity Board which provides electricity for street lights in the electric posts owned and maintained by the Board. More than one-fourth of O&M expenditure was spent on payment of water charges for street taps. The Kerala Water Authority, a public sector undertaking, provides drinking water supply in rural areas. They provide street taps based on the request of GPs and collect water charges for it. Fuel charges for vehicles and sanitation expenses are other items accounting for about 12 per cent of O&M expenditure. Another item of O&M expenditure is the repair and maintenance expenditure of vehicles, equipment, computers and other machinery of the GP. A review of the trends in the total O&M expenditure showed that it registered a growth in 2012–2013 and 2013–2014, but witnessed a negative growth in the subsequent year.

Miscellaneous Expenditure

This includes items like depreciation, drought and flood relief, compensation from own fund, interest and finance charges, the amount written off, etc. Table 4.15 gives the miscellaneous items of expenditure for a period of four years. A major item of the expenditure is depreciation, accounting for 72 per cent of the total. The other items of expenditure are drought and flood relief, amount written off and compensation from own fund.

Welfare Pensions

The GPs have been implementing a number of social welfare schemes of the state government. Here, the funds are given by the state government and the function of GPs is to distribute it to the beneficiaries. Table 4.16 gives the amount of welfare pension distributed by the GPs for a period of four years. There had been a steady increase in total amount dispersed. The amount dispersed ranged between ₹67.85 lakh and ₹174.60 lakh per year. Widow pension ranked first in terms of the

Table 4.15 *Miscellaneous Expenditure per GP: Amount, Growth Rate and Composition*

Item	2011–2012 (₹ in Thousand)	2012–2013 (₹ in Thousand)	2013–2014 (₹ in Thousand)	2014–2015 (₹ in Thousand)	2014–2015 Composition (%)
Depreciation	24.25	178.27	1,010.72	1,126.64	72.01
Drought and flood relief	27.96	92.58	143.14	240.94	15.40
Grants, contributions and compensation from own fund	20.36	10.50	29.98	57.13	3.65
Interest and finance charges	85.70	34.09	8.35	7.23	0.46
Provisions and write-off	38.87	38.01	50.03	71.45	4.57
Others	604.88	322.98	154.18	61.17	3.91
Total	**802.03**	**676.43**	**1,396.40**	**1,564.55**	**100**
Growth rate (%)		**−15.66**	**106.44**	**12.04**	

amount dispersed and accounts for 44 per cent of the total amount. Old-age pension, agricultural workers pension and disabled pension are the other important items. The other items of pension distributed were financial help given for marriage of widow's daughter, pension for unmarried women aged above 50 years, production incentives to paddy growers, unemployment allowance and other assistance.

The social welfare pension schemes were distributed by the government departments directly to the beneficiaries prior to 1996. The schemes having large number of beneficiaries were transferred to GPs, municipalities and MCs between 1996 and 2001 resulting in substantial increase in the administrative work of LGs. The work involves updating the list of pensioners, deletion and addition of beneficiaries, sending money orders, remitting the amount in bank accounts of beneficiaries, etc. The GPs also used to distribute pensions directly to the beneficiaries. The entire work was done manually till recently.

Table 4.16 *Expenditure on Welfare Pension per GP: Amount, Growth Rate and Composition*

Item	2011–2012 (₹ in Thousand)	2012–2013 (₹ in Thousand)	2013–2014 (₹ in Thousand)	2014–2015 (₹ in Thousand)	2014–2015 Composition (%)
Agricultural workers pension	2,162.16	2,128.34	2,037.12	2,858.25	16.37
Financial help for widow's daughters marriage	85.93	76.34	128.21	183.21	1.05
Destitute/Widow pension	2,193.06	4,109.56	5,023.17	7,703.06	44.12
Disabled pension	942.38	1,527.14	1,953.45	2,326.40	13.32
Old-age pension	789.50	1,773.46	1,035.00	3,515.76	20.14
Pension for unmarried women aged above 50	123.10	20.60	270.24	378.49	2.17
Production incentive to paddy growers	99.19	66.66	126.50	160.46	0.92
Unemployment allowance	279.18	286.44	149.94	256.74	1.47
Other pensions/assistance	110.56	377.16	56.22	78.06	0.44
Total	**6,785.07**	**10,551.94**	**10,779.85**	**17,460.45**	**100**
Growth rate (%)		55.52	2.16	61.97	

The available evidence suggests that the transfer of pension distribution without corresponding changes in administration and staff have adversely affected the functioning of the GPs. A study conducted for the 3rd SFC, in 50 sample GPs in Kerala, which examined the implementation of pension schemes, found that it had affected all aspects of the functioning of GPs (Prakash 2005). The GPs were entrusted with the responsibility of pension payments and average number of pensioners was 1,705 per GP (Table 4A.1). Though there had been substantial increase in the workload between 1995 and 2005, the growth in the staff was inadequate (Table 4A.2). The average number of staff increased from 12.5 in 1995 to 14.9 in 2005 (Table 4A.3). Though there had been a substantial increase in the administrative work, the growth in clerical staff such as UD and LD clerks was meagre (Table 4A.4). The study arrived at the following conclusions: (a) with the transfer of pension schemes to the GPs, there had been a major shift in their activities and the entire time, energy and resources were utilized for pension distribution; (b) the study found that heavy administrative work involved in the distribution of pension had adversely affected the mandatory and civic functions and plan activities; (c) all the GPs reported heavy work pressure for their staff due to pension distribution. They had reported that they were forced to stop other office work for many days for the distribution of the pension; (d) transfer of the major pension schemes to GPs without considering changes required in administrative set-up, additional staff, its effect on the mandatory and civic services and plan activities had created total chaos in GPs.

Centrally Sponsored Schemes

The GPs have been implementing a number of CSS. Table 4.17 gives the item-wise expenditure of CSS for a period of four years. The total expenditure on CSS per GP ranged between ₹127 lakh and ₹130 lakh. Among the CSS, MGNREGS is the single item which accounted for 85 per cent. The implementation of the scheme has also created severe strain on the administration of the GPs. A study conducted on the performance of MGNREGS based on a sample of 50 GPs in Kerala came to the conclusion that inadequate staff is a major factor contributing to unsatisfactory performance. The study identified shortage of staff namely administrative,

Table 4.17 Expenditure on CSS per GP: Amount, Growth Rate and Composition

Item	2011–2012 (₹ in Thousand)	2012–2013 (₹ in Thousand)	2013–2014 (₹ in Thousand)	2014–2015 (₹ in Thousand)	2014–2015 Composition (%)
BSUP/IHSDP	0	1.07	73.39	10.18	0.08
Flood Relief	82.16	222.06	267.78	221.74	1.71
IAY	48.12	104.32	25.03	30.23	0.23
ICDS	246.84	263.50	227.33	226.59	1.74
Kudumbashree	8.53	28.84	3.03	7.36	0.06
MP Fund	37.96	42.89	16.42	57.18	0.44
MGNREGS	10,951.70	11,954.76	11,450.21	11,010.16	84.68
NRHM/NUHM	0	0.21	0.13	0.01	0.00
SGRY	258.82	0	0	0	0.00
SGSY/SJSRY	709.15	1,006.75	637.04	812.81	6.25
SSA	124.13	81.12	198.23	126.60	0.97
Total sanitation	52.25	66.53	96.68	181.29	1.39
Other items	202.90	76.38	285.66	317.46	2.45
Total	**12,722.58**	**13,848.44**	**13,280.94**	**13,001.63**	**100**
Growth rate (%)		8.85	–4.10	–2.10	

other categories, field, data entry operators, etc., as a major reason. There had been huge dropout of data entry operators. The data entry operators appointed on temporary basis gave up the job due to low wages and heavy workload (Prakash et al. 2013). The other important items of CSS are SGSY/SJSRY, flood relief, ICDS, SSA and total sanitation. A review of the trends in total expenditure shows that there had been a negative growth of CSS during the years 2013–2014 and 2014–2015. A negative growth rate was also shown in the case of MGNREGS.

CONCLUSIONS

The central issue in the finances of GPs is the very low share of its own resources and heavy reliance on funds from the state government for its functioning. A major factor which contributed to this situation is the non-transfer of powers to LGs to effect periodical revision of taxes and non-tax items collected by them. The state government, which retained powers to revise taxes and non-taxes of LGs, had not taken steps to effect periodical revision for about two decades. In the case of property tax, which accounts for major share of tax revenue of GPs, the rate of tax was revised after a gap of 17 years. But the rate revision was practically withdrawn after two years. In the case of professional tax, which accounts for one-third of total tax revenue of GPs, the upper ceiling limit of the tax rate remained unchanged for the last 31 years (since 1988) due to inaction of the successive central governments. Another factor is the low priority given by majority of GPs to own revenue mobilization and failure to take prompt action to collect taxes, non-tax items and its arrears.

As per KPRA, 1994, the core functions of GPs are mandatory, civic and development. But a review of structure of expenditure shows that the largest share of expenditure was incurred on its agency functions such as distribution of welfare functions, implementation of MGNREGS and other CSS. This is an unhealthy development that has been taking place in Kerala's local governance. This has resulted in deterioration of its core functions such as mandatory, civic, development and maintenance of assets, thereby creating a situation in which GPs spend major share of their effort, time and manpower on non-priority agency functions neglecting core functions.

APPENDIX A

Table 4A.1 *Welfare Pension and Number of Beneficiaries (2004–2005)*

Sl No.	Welfare Pension	Number of Sample GPs	Total Number of Beneficiaries	Average Number of Beneficiaries
1	Agriculture workers	49	28,063	573
2	Unemployment assistance	48	25,932	540
3	National old-age pension	47	5,273	112
4	Destitute pension	46	12,740	277
5	Disabled and mentally retarded pension	47	8,299	177
6	Pension to unmarried women above 50 years	41	1,064	26
	Total		**81,371**	**1,705**

Source: Prakash (2005b).

Table 4A.2 *Total Number of Staff in Sample GPs*

Sl No.	District	1995		2000		2005	
		Total Number of Staff	Number of Sample GPs	Total Number of Staff	Number of Sample GPs	Total Number of Staff	Number of Sample GPs
1	Thiruvananthapuram	125	9	136	9	172	10
2	Kollam	73	5	76	5	80	5
3	Pathanamthitta	13	1	13	1	14	1
4	Alappuzha	36	4	36	4	42	4
5	Kottayam	71	6	77	6	93	6
6	Idukki	21	2	21	2	22	2
7	Ernakulam	80	7	83	7	93	7
8	Thrissur	10	1	11	1	13	1
9	Palakkad	43	4	44	4	51	4
10	Malappuram	58	4	59	4	64	4
11	Kozhikode	44	2	45	2	45	2
12	Kannur	5	1	8	1	19	2
13	Kasaragod	8	1	10	1	36	2
	Total	**587**	**47**	**619**	**47**	**744**	**50**

Source: Same as Table 4A.1.

Table 4A.3 *Average Staff Strength per GP*

Sl No.	District	Average Number of Staff in 1995	Average Number of Staff in 2000	Average Number of Staff in 2005
1	Thiruvananthapuram	13.9	15.1	17.2
2	Kollam	14.6	15.2	16.0
3	Pathanamthitta	13.0	13.0	14.0
4	Alappuzha	9.0	9.0	10.5
5	Kottayam	11.8	12.8	15.5
6	Idukki	10.5	10.5	11.0
7	Ernakulam	11.4	11.9	13.3
8	Thrissur	10.0	11.0	13.0
9	Palakkad	10.8	11.0	12.8
10	Malappuram	14.5	14.8	16.0
11	Kozhikode	22.0	22.5	22.5
12	Kannur	5.0	8.0	9.5
13	Kasaragod	8.0	10.0	18.0
	Total	**12.5**	**13.2**	**14.9**

Source: Same as Table 4A.1.

Table 4A.4 *Total Staff Strength (Category-Wise)*

Sl No.	Item	1995		2000		2005	
		Total Number of Staff	Number of Sample GPs	Total Number of Staff	Number of Sample GPs	Total Number of Staff	Number of Sample GPs
1	Secretary	42	42	44	44	49	49
2	Junior superintendent	42	42	42	42	45	45
3	UD clerk	148	47	148	46	158	49
4	Overseer	14	13	16	15	31	26
5	LD clerk	150	47	162	47	181	50
6	Librarian	23	22	24	23	31	28
7	Peon	67	46	68	47	74	50
8	Sweeper	77	32	86	35	97	40
9	Driver	7	7	8	8	16	15
10	LD clerk (redistributed)	3	3	8	8	38	36
11	Others	14	8	13	8	24	15
	Total	**587**	**47**	**619**	**47**	**744**	**50**

Source: Same as Table 4A.1.

Finances of Block and District Panchayats

The functions, responsibilities and resources assigned to BPs are much different from that of GPs. They are not assigned mandatory and civic functions or collection of taxes. BPs are entrusted with functions related to development plans, maintenance of own assets and assets of TIs, coordination of the activities of TIs, implementation of CSS, etc. For meeting the expenses related to establishment, administration, maintenance and annual plan, they solely depend on the transfer of funds from the state government. The functions assigned to DPs are similar to that of BPs. Their major functions are development plans, maintenance of own assets and assets of TIs and coordination of the activities of TIs. In this chapter, we examine the finances of BPs and DPs. The data for the study were collected from a sample of 13 BPs, selecting 1 BP each from 13 districts (Table 5.1). The sample BPs account for 9 per cent of the total BPs in Kerala.

FINANCES OF BLOCK PANCHAYATS

In this section, we discuss two aspects of finances, namely growth and structure of receipts and expenditure. The structure of receipts of BPs may be classified into four items, namely (a) transfer of funds from state resources, (b) welfare pension receipts, (c) CSS receipts and (d) borrowing. The average total receipts received per BP ranged between ₹947.11 lakh and ₹1,058.71 lakh during a period of four years. Table 5.2 gives the item-wise receipts for a period of four years between 2011–2012 and 2014–2015. A review of the trends in yearly total receipts indicates considerable fluctuations. This was due to the

Table 5.1 *Distribution of Sample Block Panchayats*

Sl No.	Name of Districts	Name of Sample BPs	Number of Total BPs	Number of Sample BPs
1	Thiruvananthapuram	Kilimanoor	11	1
2	Kollam	Vettikavala	11	1
3	Pathanamthitta	Pulikezhu	8	1
4	Alappuzha	Kanjikkuzhi	12	1
5	Kottayam	Laalam	11	1
6	Ernakulam	Pampakuda	14	1
7	Thrissur	Vellangallur	16	1
8	Palakkad	Mannarkkad	13	1
9	Malappuram	Vengara	15	1
10	Kozhikode	Kunnamangalam	12	1
11	Wayanad	Panamaram	4	1
12	Kannur	Edakkad	11	1
13	Kasaragod	Karadukka	6	1
	Total	–	**144**	**13**

carry-over of unspent amount of a year to subsequent year and delayed receipts of CSS and welfare pensions.

An examination of structure of receipts gives the following broad changes. The share of CSS receipts, which was the largest item in 2011–2012, registered a continuous decline. On the other hand, the share of transferred funds received from the state government registered a continuous increase and emerged as the major item of receipts.

The share of receipts of welfare pensions and CSS receipts was very small. A review of the trends in items of receipts indicates an increase in transfer of funds in all the years and fall in growth rate of welfare pension and CSS receipts in two out of the five years. During the year 2014–2015, BPs had not borrowed any amount from financial institutions and banks.

Table 5.2 *Total Receipts per Block Panchayats: Amount, Composition and Growth Rate*

Receipts	2011–2012	2012–2013	2013–2014	2014–2015
(₹ In Lakh)				
Total transfer of funds	275.42	288.16	386.63	490.56
Welfare pension	13.95	4.36	28.67	6.84
CSS	646.27	437.60	613.67	453.63
Borrowing	11.47	20.23	29.73	0
Total	**947.11**	**750.35**	**1,058.71**	**951.02**
Composition (%)				
Total transfer of funds	29.1	38.4	36.5	51.6
Welfare pension	1.5	0.6	2.7	0.7
CSS	68.2	58.3	58.0	47.7
Borrowing	1.2	2.7	2.8	0.0
Total	**100.0**	**100.0**	**100.0**	**100.0**
Growth (%)				
Total transfer of funds		4.6	34.2	26.9
Welfare pension		−68.7	557.2	−76.2
CSS		−32.3	40.2	−26.1
Borrowing		76.3	47.0	−100.0
Total		**−20.8**	**41.0**	**−10.2**

Devolution of Funds

The BPs received the devolved funds for four years as per the recommendations of the 4th SFC. The total amount received ranged between ₹275.42 and ₹490.56 lakh during the period of four years. Table 5.3 presents the item-wise amount received by BPs as per devolution. Development fund meant for financing annual plan of the BPs accounted for more than 84 per cent of the total transferred funds. Funds for maintenance of non-road assets of own and TIs ranged between 5.2 and 9.2 per cent of total devolved funds. The fund was given for maintenance of own assets of BPs including buildings,

Table 5.3 *Amount Received per Block Panchayat through Devolution: Amount, Composition and Growth Rate*

Category of Fund	2011– 2012 (₹ in Lakh)	2012– 2013 (₹ in Lakh)	2013– 2014 (₹ in Lakh)	2014– 2015 (₹ in Lakh)	2014–2015 Composition (%)
General purpose	16.30	20.00	24.09	28.00	5.7
Development (excluding World Bank assistance)	241.33	243.31	328.64	417.66	85.1
Maintenance (road)	3.37	4.30	0.45	0	0.0
Maintenance (non-road)	14.42	20.55	33.45	44.90	9.2
Total	275.42	288.16	386.63	490.56	100
Growth rate (%)		4.6	34.2	26.9	

vehicles, equipment, etc., and assets of TIs like health centres, taluk hospitals, other health institutions, care homes, old-age homes, etc. As BPs do not have much roads under their jurisdiction, the receipts of road maintenance is small. GPF was another item of transferred fund and accounted for 5.7 to 6.9 per cent of total devolved funds. The fund is given for meeting the establishment, administration and miscellaneous expenditure.

Centrally Sponsored Schemes

The BPs execute agency functions such as implementation of CSS of the Union Government. Among the CSS, the IAY was the major item accounting for more than half of the total receipts (Table 5.4). The scheme, a rural housing scheme, is meant to provide financial support for poor people for constructing houses. The scheme which was renamed as Pradhan Mantri Awas Yojana - Gramin (PMAY-G) aims at providing a pukka house, with basic amenities, to all houseless households and those households living in kutcha and dilapidated houses, by 2022. The minimum size of the house is 25 sq. mt with a hygienic cooking space. The unit assistance has been increased from ₹70,000 to ₹1.20 lakh in plain and from ₹75,000 to ₹1.30 lakh in hilly

Table 5.4 *CSS Receipts per Block Panchayat*

	2011–2012 (₹ in Lakh)	2012–2013 (₹ in Lakh)	2013–2014 (₹ in Lakh)	2014–2015 (₹ in Lakh)	2014–2015 Composition (%)
Flood relief	3.39	1.07	0	0.61	0.13
IAY	194.58	247.22	424.94	240.63	53.04
ICDS	4.37	1.50	0.28	0.05	0.01
MP Fund	3.46	7.23	15.04	12.64	2.79
MGNREGS	388.52	97.12	0.67	41.12	9.07
Total sanitation	3.73	3.60	8.72	15.42	3.40
NABARD	1.76	0.27	0	0	0.00
SGSY/SJSRY	11.74	7.02	3.16	0.71	0.16
Others	34.72	72.57	160.86	142.45	31.40
Total	**646.27**	**437.60**	**613.67**	**453.63**	**100**
Growth rate (%)		**−32.3**	**40.2**	**−26.1**	

states, difficult areas and integrated action plan (IAP) districts. The other major schemes are MGNREGS, total sanitation and Member of Parliament fund meant for implementing local development projects.

Growth and Structure of Expenditure

The expenditure is classified into eight items, namely administration, CSS, annual plan, establishment, maintenance, O&M, welfare pension and miscellaneous. The total expenditure per BP ranged between ₹744.70 lakh and ₹1,187.64 lakh during the period of four years. Table 5.5 presents the item-wise and total expenditure per BP for a period of four years. An analysis of structure of expenditure gives the following changes. CSS expenditure, which was the largest item of expenditure during 2011–2012, registered a decline in its share in the subsequent years. This may be attributed to the distribution of major share of MGNREGS directly to the GPs and decline in amounts of certain other items of CSS. There had been a substantial increase in share of expenditure of annual plan. The share increased from 32.2 per cent

Table 5.5 *Total Expenditure per Block Panchayat: Amount, Composition and Growth Rate*

Item of Expenditure	2011–2012	2012–2013	2013–2014	2014–2015
(₹ in Lakh)				
Administrative	11.87	6.55	9.39	8.27
CSS	470.55	294.30	298.26	351.86
Decentralized plan programme	265.56	408.95	794.71	655.61
Establishment	7.54	7.62	10.73	11.94
Maintenance	31.70	13.17	49.01	33.68
Miscellaneous	29.39	3.81	5.76	44.28
O&M	8.67	10.11	19.60	8.88
Welfare pension	0	0.20	0.16	0.46
Total	**825.29**	**744.70**	**1,187.64**	**1,114.98**
Composition (%)				
Administrative	1.4	0.9	0.8	0.7
CSS	57.0	39.5	25.1	31.6
Decentralized plan programme	32.2	54.9	66.9	58.8
Establishment	0.9	1.0	0.9	1.1
Maintenance	3.8	1.8	4.1	3.0
Miscellaneous	3.6	0.5	0.5	4.0
O&M	1.1	1.4	1.7	0.8
Welfare pension	0.0	0.0	0.0	0.0
Total	**100.0**	**100.0**	**100.0**	**100.0**
Growth (%)				
Administrative	–	–44.8	43.4	–12.0
CSS	–	–37.5	1.3	18.0
Decentralized plan programme	–	54.0	94.3	–17.5
Establishment	–	1.1	41.1	11.1

(Continued)

Table 5.5 *(Continued)*

Item of Expenditure	2011–2012	2012–2013	2013–2014	2014–2015
Maintenance	–	–58.5	272.1	–31.3
Miscellaneous	–	–87.1	51.5	668.4
O&M	–	16.5	93.9	–54.7
Welfare pension	–	0.0	–21.1	190.7
Total	**–**	**–9.8**	**59.5**	**–6.1**

in 2011–2012 to 58.8 per cent in 2014–2015. Miscellaneous, maintenance and establishment are other items of expenditure.

A review of growth in total expenditure of BPs indicates the following trend. CSS expenditure registered a large fall in 2012–2013 followed by an increase in subsequent years. There had been a substantial growth in annual plan expenditure in the first two years followed by a fall in its growth rate. There was much variation in other items of expenditure such as administration, maintenance, miscellaneous and O&M. The yearly variation in growth of expenditure may be due to spending of balance amount of a financial year in the subsequent year and delayed receipts of other items like CSS.

Annual Plan Expenditure

BPs used to prepare annual plans for development based on plan formulation guidelines of the state government. The sector-wise division of the plan expenditure are infrastructure, production, service and others not included in sector classification. The total plan expenditure per BP ranged between ₹265.56 and ₹794.71 lakh. Table 5.6 gives annual plan expenditure, its composition and growth for a period of five years. An analysis of the structure of expenditure indicates the following pattern of changes: (a) the share of service sector plan expenditure witnessed a substantial increase (37.2 to 80.3%). This shows a substantial shift in allocation of plan funds from infrastructure and production sectors to service sector; (b) a disturbing development has

Table 5.6 *Decentralized Plan per Block Panchayat: Amount, Composition and Growth Rate*

Sector	2011–2012 (₹ in Lakh)	2012–2013 (₹ in Lakh)	2013–2014 (₹ in Lakh)	2014–2015 (₹ in Lakh)	2014–2015 Composition (%)
Infrastructure	63.26	58.10	50.58	86.75	13.2
Productive	43.83	27.75	33.34	34.57	5.3
Projects not included in sector division	59.64	3.31	4.24	7.55	1.2
Service	98.83	319.79	706.57	526.73	80.3
Total	**265.56**	**408.95**	**794.71**	**655.61**	**100.0**
Growth rate (%)		**54.0**	**94.3**	**–17.5**	

been the steep fall in the share of productive sector expenditure such as agriculture and industry; (c) another unhealthy change has been fall in the share of infrastructure sector; (d) the share of expenditure not included in any of the aforementioned sectors also registered a substantial fall; (e) thus, the overall change in the structure of expenditure indicates an unhealthy shift from production and infrastructure sectors to service sector.

A review of the trend in expenditure shows that there had been an increase in the growth of plan expenditure during first two years followed by negative growth in the third year. There were also wide variations in growth of expenditure in all the four sectors.

Maintenance Expenditure

Funds are devolved for meeting maintenance of road and non-road assets of the BPs as well as assets of TIs. Table 5.7 gives maintenance expenditure incurred by BPs. A noticeable feature is that more than 99 per cent of maintenance fund was spent for non-road assets in 2011–2012. This is due to the fact that BPs do not have public roads under their jurisdiction.

Table 5.7 *Maintenance Expenditure per Block Panchayat*

Category	2011–2012 (₹ in Lakh)	2012–2013 (₹ in Lakh)	2013–2014 (₹ in Lakh)	2014–2015 (₹ in Lakh)	2014–2015 Composition (%)
Non-road assets	31.41	12.24	39.23	29.04	86.22
Road assets	0.29	0.93	9.78	4.64	13.78
Total	31.70	13.17	49.01	33.68	100
Growth rate (%)		–58.5	272.1	–31.3	

CSS

The BPs have been implementing a number of CSS like IAY, Member of Parliament Fund, MGNREGS, total sanitation, etc. Table 5.8 gives the item-wise expenditure of CSS for a period of four years. The total expenditure on CSS per BP ranged between ₹294.3 lakh and ₹470.5 lakh. Among the items of CSS, the major item is IAY. But the implementation of IAY created additional financial burden to BPs. As per the IAY scheme, the central government was giving ₹70,000

Table 5.8 *CSS Expenditure per Block Panchayat*

Category	2011–2012 (₹ in Lakh)	2012–2013 (₹ in Lakh)	2013–2014 (₹ in Lakh)	2014–2015 (₹ in Lakh)	2014–2015 Composition (%)
Flood relief	2.25	0.96	0	1.21	0.34
IAY	193.51	155.16	250.81	245.32	69.72
ICDS	0.03	0	0	0.01	0.42
MP Fund	1.86	5.00	15.08	12.64	3.59
MGNREGS	245.45	97.10	0.43	40.92	11.63
SGSY/SJSRY	14.47	5.05	3.14	0.46	0.13
Total sanitation	2.58	4.06	2.59	7.32	2.08
Other items	7.42	26.97	25.35	42.53	12.09
Total	470.55	294.30	298.26	351.86	100
Growth rate (%)	–	–37.5	1.3	18.0	–

as financial assistance per beneficiary. But the state government had enhanced the amount to ₹1.5 lakh per beneficiary. The government asked the BPs to bear the additional financial burden either from the development fund or through borrowing. Due to this, amount of fund allotted to annual plan was forced to be diverted to the IAY scheme. Some of the BPs borrowed money from commercial banks to finance the additional amount as per the directive of the state government. The BPs complained that the state government has not given the amount and they had to undergo financial problems. A major complaint raised by the sample BPs was that the state government imposed certain state schemes and modified central schemes and asked them to spend money from their development fund. The examples they cited were Elamkulam Manakkal Sankaran Namboodiripad (Former Chief Minister of Kerala) EMS housing scheme and enhancement of IAY share. It may be pointed out that this type of intervention of the state government is against the principles of transfer of powers and functions, decentralized planning process and fiscal decentralization.

FINANCES OF DISTRICT PANCHAYATS

In this part, we examine the finances of DPs. The data for the study were collected from all the DPs except Palakkad (Table 5.9). The functions assigned to DPs are similar to that of BPs, such as formulation and implementation of annual plans, maintenance of own assets and assets of TIs and coordination of the activities of TIs. Here, we examine two aspects of the finances, namely growth and structure of receipts and expenditure.

The structure of receipts of DPs may be classified into four items, namely (a) transfer of funds from state resources; (b) welfare pension receipts, (c) CSS receipts and (d) borrowing. The average total receipts received per DP ranged between ₹3,664 and ₹6,581 lakh during a period of four years. Table 5.10 gives the item-wise receipts for a period of four years between 2011–2012 and 2014–2015. A review of the trend in yearly total receipts indicates considerable fluctuations. This was due to carry-over of unspent amount of a year to the subsequent year and delayed receipts of CSS, welfare pensions and variations in borrowing.

Table 5.9 *Distribution of District Panchayats*

Sl No.	Name of Districts
1	Thiruvananthapuram
2	Kollam
3	Pathanamthitta
4	Alappuzha
5	Kottayam
6	Idukki
7	Ernakulam
8	Thrissur
9	Malappuram
10	Kozhikode
11	Wayanad
12	Kannur
13	Kasaragod

Table 5.10 *Total Receipts per District Panchayat: Amount, Composition and Growth Rate*

Receipts	2011–2012	2012–2013	2013–2014	2014–2015
(₹ in Lakh)				
Total transfer of funds	3,355.02	3,657.18	5,868.92	6,399.77
Welfare pension	11.90	23.48	20.41	21.85
CSS	134.96	103.18	242.32	159.93
Borrowing	162.25	0.96	49.74	0
Total	**3,664.12**	**3,787.81**	**6,181.39**	**6,581.54**
Composition (%)				
Total transfer of funds	91.6	96.6	94.9	97.2
Welfare pension	0.3	0.7	0.3	0.3
CSS	3.7	2.7	3.9	204
Borrowing	4.4	0.0	0.8	0.0
Total	**100.0**	**100.0**	**100.0**	**100.0**

Receipts	2011–2012	2012–2013	2013–2014	2014–2015
		Growth (%)		
Total transfer of funds		9.0	60.5	9.0
Welfare pension		122.5	–22.9	7.0
CSS		–23.5	134.8	–34.0
Borrowing		–99.4	5,083.6	–100.0
Total		**3.4**	**63.2**	**6.5**

A review of the structure of receipts shows that the transfer of funds from the state government such as GPF, maintenance fund and development fund accounted for more than 91 per cent of the total receipts. It ranged between 91 and 97 per cent. The other three items of receipts are welfare pension, CSS and borrowing. A review of the trends in growth of receipts indicates that the only item which registered a growth in three years was transferred funds.

Devolution of Funds

The DPs received the devolved funds for four years as per the recommendations of the 4th SFC. The total amount received ranged between ₹3,355 and ₹6,399 lakh during the period of four years. Table 5.11 presents the item-wise amount received per DP as per devolution. Development fund meant for financing annual plan of the DP was the largest item of devolved funds. Funds given for the maintenance of district roads under the jurisdiction of DPs was the second major item of funds. It accounted from 21.8 to 24.8 per cent. The third major item is the maintenance fund given for maintaining the own assets of the DPs and TIs like district agriculture farm, minor irrigation projects, water supply schemes of DPs, veterinary centres and related units, fisheries schools, upper primary schools, high schools, higher secondary schools, technical schools, vocational training institutions, district hospitals, post-matric hostels, etc. The fourth item is the GPF meant for meeting the expenditure on administration, establishment and miscellaneous expenditure. The share of the GPF ranged between 3.4 and 7.8 per cent of the total transferred funds.

Table 5.11 *Amount Received per District Panchayat through Devolution: Amount, Composition and Growth Rate*

Category of Fund	2011–2012 (₹ in Lakh)	2012–2013 (₹ in Lakh)	2013–2014 (₹ in Lakh)	2014–2015 (₹ in Lakh)	2014–2015 Composition (%)
General purpose	115.38	285.70	417.37	451.44	7.1
Development (excluding World Bank assistance and 13th FC grant)	2,313.52	2,292.16	3,499.17	3,951.20	61.7
Maintenance (road)	732.87	810.30	1,457.59	1,398.10	21.8
Maintenance (non-road)	193.24	269.01	494.78	599.03	9.4
Total	3,355.02	3,657.18	5,868.92	6,399.77	100.0
Growth rate (%)	–	9.0	60.5	9.0	

A review of the growth in the total receipts shows wide fluctuations. The items which registered a growth in all the three years are GPF and maintenance fund given for non-road item.

Centrally Sponsored Schemes

The DPs receive only a small amount as CSS receipts (Table 5.12). The total CSS receipts ranged between ₹103.18 lakh and ₹242.32 lakh. National Bank for Agriculture and Rural development (NABARD) assistance was a major item of receipts during the year 2014–2015. The other items are SSA, total sanitation and others.

Growth and Structure of Expenditure

The expenditure is classified into eight items, namely administration, CSS, annual plan, establishment, maintenance, O&M, welfare pension and miscellaneous. The total expenditure per DP ranged between ₹3,399 and ₹5,995 lakh during the period between 2011–2012 and

Table 5.12 *CSS Receipts per District Panchayat*

Item	2011–2012 (₹ in Lakh)	2012–2013 (₹ in Lakh)	2013–2014 (₹ in Lakh)	2014–2015 (₹ in Lakh)	2014–2015 Composition (%)
Flood relief	0	0	3.82	0	0.00
MP Fund	9.94	2.30	1.34	0	0.00
SSA	26.57	8.14	9.45	7.28	4.55
Total sanitation	0.16	5.14	1.70	1.81	1.13
NABARD assistance	0.70	0	40.44	80.12	50.10
Others	97.59	87.60	189.36	70.72	44.22
Total	134.96	103.18	242.32	159.93	100
Growth rate (%)		−23.5	134.8	−34.0	

2014–2015. Table 5.13 presents the item-wise and total expenditure per DP for a period of four years. An analysis of the structure of expenditure reveals the following. Annual plan expenditure is the largest item of expenditure accounting for more than 56 per cent of the total expenditure. There had been a decline in its share between 2011–2012 and 2014–2015. Maintenance expenditure, the second largest item, witnessed an increase in its share. It accounted for one-third of the total expenditure in 2014–2015. Thus, formulation and implementation of annual development of plan for the local-level development and maintenance of road and non-road assets are the main activities of DPs. The other items of expenditure such as administration, establishment and miscellaneous account for a small share. The share of expenditure on CSS and welfare pension was only 1.2 per cent in 2014–2015.

A review of the growth in total expenditure shows much variation. This fluctuation may be due to the spending of the balance amount of the transferred funds in the subsequent year due to non-completion of annual plan projects and delayed receipts of funds. The practice followed is to spend money of uncompleted plan projects of a financial year in subsequent years as spill-over projects. But the items such as administration and establishment registered an increase in all the three years.

Table 5.13 *Total Expenditure per District Panchayat: Amount, Composition and Growth Rate*

Item of Expenditure	2011–2012	2012–2013	2013–2014	2014–2015
	(₹ in Lakh)			
Administrative	36.74	46.41	57.86	74.64
CSS	72.19	34.01	35.62	43.56
Decentralized plan programme	2,862.85	2,386.06	3,293.36	3,530.30
Establishment	137.29	142.68	162.56	175.04
Maintenance	637.42	605.13	2,031.53	1,988.76
Miscellaneous	100.38	148.87	184.78	129.24
O&M	74.19	18.61	48.01	24.69
Welfare pension	15.84	17.33	21.88	29.53
Total	**3,936.90**	**3,399.10**	**5,835.60**	**5,995.77**
	Composition (%)			
Administrative	0.9	1.4	1.0	1.2
CSS	1.8	1.0	0.6	0.7
Decentralized plan programme	72.7	70.2	56.4	58.9
Establishment	3.5	4.2	2.8	2.9
Maintenance	16.2	17.8	34.8	33.2
Miscellaneous	2.5	4.4	3.2	2.2
O&M	1.9	0.5	0.8	0.4
Welfare pension	0.4	0.5	0.4	0.5
Total	**100.0**	**100.0**	**100.0**	**100.0**
	Growth (%)			
Administrative		26.3	24.7	29.0
CSS		−52.9	4.7	22.3
Decentralized plan programme		−16.7	38.0	7.2
Establishment		3.9	13.9	7.7
Maintenance		−5.1	235.7	−2.1
Miscellaneous		48.3	24.1	−30.1
O&M		−74.9	158.0	−48.6
Welfare pension		9.4	26.2	35.0
Total		**−13.7**	**71.7**	**2.7**

Annual Plan Expenditure

DPs used to prepare annual plans for development of districts based on plan formulation guidelines of the state government. The sector-wise division of the plan expenditure are infrastructure, production, service and others not included in sector classification. The total plan expenditure per DP ranged between ₹2,386 and ₹3,530 lakh. Table 5.14 gives annual plan expenditure, its composition and growth for a period of four years. An analysis of the structure of expenditure indicates the following pattern of changes: (a) the DPs are giving high priority to service sector and its share had witnessed a substantial increase. More than half of the total plan expenditure was spent for services in all the four years except 2011–2012; (b) there was not much variation in the share of expenditure on infrastructure. The share ranged between 32 and 36 per cent of plan expenditure; (c) a disturbing and unhealthy change that has been taken place was the continuous decline in the share of the productive sector. Neglect of productive sector in plan allocation and expenditure is an important issue in DPs as well as BPs. This is a serious issue which needs urgent attention and correction; (d) the share of expenditure in projects not included in the sector division also registered a steep fall. Thus, we have to conclude that an unhealthy shift in allocation of resources has been taking place from production sector to service sector.

Table 5.14 *Decentralized Plan Programme per District Panchayat: Amount, Composition and Growth Rate*

Sector	2011–2012 (₹ in Lakh)	2012–2013 (₹ in Lakh)	2013–2014 (₹ in Lakh)	2014–2015 (₹ in Lakh)	2014–2015 Composition (%)
Infrastructure	1,015.25	769.17	1,118.55	1,283.05	36.3
Productive	350.29	262.04	319.32	299.59	8.5
Projects not included in sector division	268.21	12.98	18.09	52.27	1.5
Service	1,229.11	1,341.86	9,529.69	1,895.38	53.7
Total	**2,862.85**	**2,386.06**	**3,293.36**	**3,530.30**	**100.0**
Growth rate (%)	–	**–16.7**	**38.0**	**7.2**	

A review of the trend in expenditure shows that there had been a fall in growth in total plan expenditure during 2012–2013. But during the subsequent years, plan expenditure registered a growth. An unhealthy development was the fall in the growth rate of productive sectors in all years except one year.

Maintenance Expenditure

Funds are devolved for meeting maintenance of road and non-road assets of the DPs as well as assets of TIs. Table 5.15 gives the item-wise maintenance expenditure incurred. Expenditure on maintenance of roads accounts for three-fourths of the total maintenance expenditure. The expenditure on this item was sizeable due to the responsibility of DPs to conduct periodical maintenance and upgradation of district roads under their jurisdiction. Though DPs are entrusted with the responsibility of maintenance of a large number of transferred medical, educational and other institutions, the share of the expenditure was about one-fourth of the total maintenance expenditure. A review of growth showed that there existed wide variations in total expenditure.

CONCLUSION

The analysis of the finances of BPs and DPs may be concluded with the following observations. The functions, responsibilities and resources assigned to BPs are much different from that of GPs. They are not

Table 5.15 *Maintenance Expenditure per District Panchayat*

Category	2011–2012 (₹ in Lakh)	2012–2013 (₹ in Lakh)	2013–2014 (₹ in Lakh)	2014–2015 (₹ in Lakh)	2014–2015 Composition (%)
Non-road assets	209.78	152.49	423.27	463.13	23.29
Road assets	427.64	452.64	1,608.26	1,525.64	76.71
Total	637.42	605.13	2,031.53	1,988.76	100
Growth rate (%)	–	–5.1	235.7	–2.1	–

assigned mandatory and civic functions or collection of taxes. BPs are entrusted with functions related to development plans, maintenance of own assets and assets of TIs, coordination of the activities of TIs, implementation of CSS, etc. For meeting the expenses related to establishment, administration, maintenance and annual plan, they solely depend on the transfer of funds from the state government. The functions assigned to DPs are similar to that of BPs.

The two items which account for 99 per cent of the total receipts of BPs are devolved funds and CSS receipts. Among the transferred funds, about 85 per cent is received as development fund for implementing annual plan. An unhealthy development that has been taking place with regard to structure of plan expenditure is the shift from infra-structure and production to service sector. Regarding maintenance, BPs spent 80 to 99 per cent of maintenance expenditure for mainte-nance of non-road assets of own and TIs. The policy of transferring the financial burden of some schemes to BPs by the state government and asking them to pay from the development fund or through bor-rowing has adversely affected the implementation of annual plans and created severe fiscal problems.

The functions assigned to DPs are similar to that of BPs. The main source of receipts of DPs are devolved funds from the state govern-ment. It ranged between 91 and 97 per cent of the total receipts. Formulation and implementation of annual plans and maintenance of road and non-road assets are the main activities of DPs. The wide fluctuations in total expenditure of DPs may be attributed to spend-ing the balance amount in subsequent year due to non-completion of annual plan projects and delayed receipts of funds. A disturbing and unhealthy change that had been taking place in plan spending was a shift of allocation of resources from productive sector to service sector. Neglect of productive sector in plan allocation and expenditure is an important issue in the development plans of DPs. Poor utiliza-tion of annual plan outlay is a major problem of the DPs. In the case of utilization of maintenance fund, DPs give high priority for roads compared to non-road assets.

Finances of Municipalities

This chapter examines the finances of municipalities in Kerala. The data for the study were collected from a sample of 14 municipalities belonging to all districts of Kerala using a structured schedule (Table 6.1). The profile of the sample municipalities is shown in Table 6.2. The study examines the growth and structure of receipts as well as expenditure. It also presents major problems and issues of municipalities pertaining to local finance. The chapter is divided into two sections, namely growth and structure of receipts and expenditure.

The urban LGs, namely municipalities and MCs in Kerala, function within the framework of KMA, 1994. The state government controlled the activities of urban LGs through a host of rules, regulations and restrictions. Though powers are given to take disciplinary action against the staff, the municipalities were not given power to appoint, terminate staff, decide wage, working conditions, etc. The staff of the urban LGs are government staff and their transfer and postings are done by the state government. The urban LGs are not given power to revise taxes, fees and user charges collected by them.

GROWTH AND STRUCTURE OF RECEIPTS

The structure of total receipts of municipalities can be classified into five items, namely (a) tax and non-tax revenue, (b) transfer of funds from the state resources, (c) the World Bank loan and 13th UFC grants, (c) CSS and welfare pension receipts and (e) borrowings. Major items of tax collected by municipalities are property tax, profession tax, entertainment tax, advertisement tax and other items. Important items of non-tax revenue collected by municipalities are building

Table 6.1 Distribution of Sample Municipalities

Sl No.	Name of Districts	Name of Sample Municipalities	Number of Sample Municipalities	Total Number of Municipalities	Sample Size (%)
1	Thiruvananthapuram	Nedumangad	1	4	25.0
2	Kollam	Karunagappalli	1	4	25.0
3	Pathanamthitta	Thiruvalla	1	4	25.0
4	Alappuzha	Alappuzha	1	6	16.6
5	Kottayam	Kottayam	1	6	16.6
6	Idukki	Thodupuzha	1	2	50.0
7	Ernakulam	North Paravur	1	13	7.7
8	Thrissur	Kunnamkulam	1	7	14.3
9	Palakkad	Shoranur	1	7	14.3
10	Malappuram	Manjeri	1	12	8.3
11	Kozhikode	Vatakara	1	7	14.3
12	Wayanad	Kalpetta	1	3	33.3
13	Kannur	Payyanur	1	9	11.1
14	Kasaragod	Kasaragod	1	3	33.3
	Total		14	87	16.1

Table 6.2 Profile of Sample Municipalities

Sl No.	Name of Sample Municipalities	Area (in Sq. Km)	Total Population (Number)	Average Own Revenue (Five Years Average) (₹ in Lakh)	Length of Road (in Km)
1	Nedumangad	32.53	60,161	283.08	107.66
2	Karunagappalli	18.65	49,604	106.26	182.00
3	Thiruvalla	27.15	52,883	586.42	300.00
4	Alappuzha	46.71	174,176	828.05	300.00
5	Kottayam	50.14	138,283	1,637.14	222.81
6	Thodupuzha	35.43	52,045	447.19	147.45
7	North Paravur	9.02	31,503	321.30	110.41
8	Kunnamkulam	34.18	54,071	479.39	141.95
9	Shoranur	32.28	43,533	300.91	289.33
10	Manjeri	53.10	97,102	425.84	212.63
11	Vatakara	21.32	75,295	679.19	135.56
12	Kalpetta	40.74	31,580	324.40	81.58
13	Payyanur	54.63	72,111	398.93	203.44
14	Kasaragod	16.69	54,172	552.53	79.83

permit fee, rent on buildings, D&O license, fines and penalties, sale of sand, market fee for public market and other items. We have already attempted a detailed analysis on the taxes and non-tax items collected, problems and major issues of LGs in Chapter 3.

We may start the analysis with an examination of the growth and structure of total receipts. For the analysis, we have used the total and item-wise receipts per municipality. The average total receipts received per municipality ranged between ₹1,599.07 lakh and ₹2,174.33 lakh between 2011–2012 and 2014–2015. Table 6.3 gives the growth and structure of the receipts of municipalities for a period of four years. A review of the trends in growth of total receipts indicates considerable yearly fluctuations. The item which witnessed a fall in growth in one year are tax, total transfer of funds, the World Bank loan and borrowings. The items such as non-tax revenue and CSS receipts registered a fall in two out of the three years. The wide variations in yearly total receipts were due to the carry-over of unspent amount of a year to subsequent year and the delayed receipts.

An analysis of the structure of receipts gives the following broad changes of individual items. The share of tax revenue ranged between 17.9 and 21.4 per cent during the period. The non-tax revenue accounted for 8.4 to 12.6 per cent. The transfer of funds from the SOTR comprising GPF, maintenance fund and development fund ranged between 37.9 and 40.7 per cent. The World Bank loan and grants from 13th UFC accounts for 8.4 to 13.8 per cent. The funds received from the CSS from the Union Government accounts for 4 to 11 per cent of the total receipts. The social welfare pensions of the state government, distributed through the municipalities, accounts for 7.7 to 13.7 per cent of the total receipts. The amount of funds received through borrowing was very small and not even accounted for 1 per cent of the total receipts.

Thus, the broad structure of revenue of municipalities indicates the following. The transfer of funds from state resources accounts for the largest share (38 to 41%) of receipts. The second major item is tax and non-tax receipts accounting for 26 to 32 per cent of total receipts. The third, fourth and fifth items are welfare pension receipts, 13th UFC

Table 6.3 *Total Receipts per Municipality: Amount, Composition and Growth Rate*

Receipts	2011–2012	2012–2013	2013–2014	2014–2015
₹ in Lakh				
Tax	310.52	346.39	465.87	387.76
Non-tax	202.21	151.20	216.18	181.81
Total transfer of funds	650.05	660.48	883.73	822.15
World Bank loan	30.24	57.88	27.09	72.08
13th UFC grants	104.30	170.14	180.36	226.33
Welfare pensions	122.65	188.54	214.49	296.76
CSS	178.03	65.17	182.06	163.82
Borrowing	1.08	9.44	4.56	20.10
Total	**1,599.07**	**1,649.25**	**2,174.33**	**2,170.81**
Composition (%)				
Tax	19.4	21.0	21.4	17.9
Non-tax	12.6	9.2	9.9	8.4
Total transfer of funds	40.7	40.0	40.6	37.9
World Bank loan	1.9	3.5	1.2	3.3
13th UFC grants	6.5	10.3	8.3	10.4
Welfare pensions	7.7	11.4	9.9	13.7
CSS	11.1	4.0	8.4	7.5
Borrowing	0.1	0.6	0.2	0.9
Total	**100.0**	**100.0**	**100.0**	**100.0**
Growth (%)				
Tax		11.6	34.5	−16.8
Non-tax		−25.2	43.0	−15.9
Total transfer of funds		1.6	33.8	−7.0
World Bank loan		91.4	−53.2	166.1
13th UFC grants		63.1	6.0	25.5
Welfare pensions		53.7	13.8	38.4
CSS		−63.4	179.4	−10.0
Borrowing		771.9	−51.6	340.4
Total		**3.1**	**31.8**	**−0.2**

grant and CSS receipts, respectively. Though there is considerable scope for borrowings, the municipalities have not exercised the option.

Tax Revenue

Property tax is the most important tax levied by municipalities. The tax accounts for 46 per cent of the share of the total taxes collected by the municipalities in 2014–2015 (Table 6.4). Before coming into the system of calculating property tax based on plinth area, the tax was assessed on annual rental value basis from April 1993. The KMA, 1994, envisaged quinquennial revision of property tax but it could not be operationalized due to non-formulation of rules in this regard. Owing to laxity on the part of the state government, revision of property tax at the expiry of every five years could not be undertaken. This led to huge financial loss for municipalities and MCs. However, the government issued rules to switch over property tax assessment from annual rental value basis to plinth area basis from April 2013.

Most of the urban LGs started revision of property tax after a long gap of 20 years. In our discussion with the municipalities, it is pointed out that they require at least one year's administrative work to switch over to the plinth area-wise system of assessment. In the meantime, the government, through an executive order in April 2015, went back from the revision. As per the new order, all houses with a plinth area

Table 6.4 *Tax Revenue per Municipality: Amount, Composition and Growth Rate*

Item of Tax	2011– 2012 (₹ in Lakh)	2012– 2013 (₹ in Lakh)	2013– 2014 (₹ in Lakh)	2014– 2015 (₹ in Lakh)	2014–2015 Composition (%)
Profession	122.06	133.55	235.94	160.92	41.5
Property	154.58	169.17	181.83	179.70	46.3
Entertainment	29.71	38.32	40.85	39.00	10.1
Advertisement	2.38	2.86	3.82	2.68	0.7
Other	1.80	2.49	3.42	5.46	1.4
Total	310.52	346.39	465.87	387.76	100.0
Growth rate (%)		11.6	34.5	−16.8	

up to 660 sq. feet have been exempted from payment of taxes and the increase in tax hike was limited to 25 per cent in the case of houses with a plinth area up to 2,000 sq. feet. The enormous administrative work done by the municipalities to switch over to plinth area-wise assessment became a futile and they stopped the revision work. Due to this, there has been a decline in the growth rate of tax since 2012–2013 (Table 6.4).

The situation is not different in case of profession tax, the second major tax collected by the municipalities. The tax accounted for 41.5 per cent of the total tax revenue of the municipalities in 2014–2015. There was wide fluctuation in the growth rate of tax between 2011–2012 and 2014–2015 (Table 6.4). A serious issue of the tax is the lack of revision of the ceiling amount of the tax since 1988. The ceiling amount of the profession tax was fixed as ₹2,500 per year per person in 1988. Though the successive UFCs had recommended a revision of the ceiling of the tax, no action has been taken by the Government of India to revise the tax since 1988. The 14th UFC had examined this issue and recommended to raise the ceiling from ₹2,500 to ₹12,000 per annum.

Another issue is poor collection of tax due to incomplete data on taxpayers, the attitude of many categories of professionals not to pay the tax and administrative and legal problems in initiating revenue recovery proceedings. The discussion with the municipalities reveals that they give very low priority for collection of the tax and bringing more taxpayers in the tax net.

Entertainment tax is the third major item of tax of the municipalities. There has been a steady decline in the growth rate of the tax. It accounted for 9 to 11 per cent of the total tax collected by the municipalities (Table 6.4). The tax is collected as per the Kerala Local Authorities Entertainments Tax Act, 1961. The tax is levied on events such as exhibition, performance, amusement, game, sport or race for which persons are admitted on payment. Entertainment tax from cinema halls was a major source of revenue of municipalities in the past. But there has been a decline in this tax revenue due to the closure of a large number of cinema halls due to unprecedented technological development in entertainment media. A disturbing development is the deletion of the entertainment tax from the list of tax collected by LGs. With the introduction of GST from July 2017, the entertainment tax is included in GST.

Non-tax Revenue

The non-tax revenue of municipalities comprises of building permit fee, rents, D&O license fee, fines, revenue from sale of land, market fee for public market and other items. The item-wise non-tax revenue collected by the municipalities for a period of four years is shown in Table 6.5. The rent from the buildings, public halls, commercial centres, etc., owned by the municipalities is the single largest items of non-tax revenue. It accounted for 37 per cent of the total non-tax revenue of municipalities. Building permit fee collected for issuing permits for construction of various types of buildings like houses, flats, commercial buildings, hospitals, schools, factories, etc., is the second major item of non-tax revenue. Fines and penalties, license fee collected under the head D&O license, revenue from the sale of

Table 6.5 *Non-tax Revenue per Municipality: Amount, Composition and Growth Rate*

Item	2011– 2012 (₹ in Lakh)	2012– 2013 (₹ in Lakh)	2013– 2014 (₹ in Lakh)	2014– 2015 (₹ in Lakh)	2014–2015 Composition (%)
Building permit fee	26.10	20.66	47.22	31.63	17.4
Rent on buildings	85.38	63.38	87.49	66.68	36.7
D&O license	8.36	11.84	12.24	9.31	5.1
Fines/Penalties	10.39	8.91	15.06	10.35	5.7
Sale of sand	6.09	7.87	9.66	7.92	4.4
Market fee for public market	2.49	2.57	3.10	3.01	1.7
Other non-taxes	63.40	35.98	41.40	52.90	29.0
Total	**202.21**	**151.20**	**216.18**	**181.81**	**100**
Growth rate (%)		**–25.2**	**43.0**	**–15.9**	

land and market fee collected from public markets are the other items of non-tax revenue.

Arrears of Tax and Non-tax

Table 6.6 gives item-wise arrears of tax and non-tax of the sample municipalities for two years, namely 2011–2012 and 2014–2015. Property tax accounted for the largest share of arrears in 2014–2015 (57%). Rent on building, profession tax and D&O license fee are the other items having largest share of arrears in 2014–2015. The items such as advertisement tax, building permit fee, entertainment tax, fines and penalties account for 1.2 per cent of the total arrears. The trends in arrears between 2011–2012 and 2014–2015 gives the following pattern of changes. On the one hand, there had been a decline in the amount of arrears of property tax, profession tax, rent on buildings and advertisement tax. On the other, there had been an increase in

Table 6.6 *Tax and Non-tax Arrears per Municipality in 2011–2012 and 2014–2015*

	2011–2012		2014–2015	
Item	*Amount ₹ in Lakh*	*Composition (%)*	*Amount ₹ in Lakh*	*Composition (%)*
Property tax	157.89	31.6	146.80	56.7
Profession tax	75.29	15.1	14.84	5.7
Rent on buildings (including shopping complex fee)	38.17	7.6	18.78	7.2
Advertisement	7.14	1.4	0.45	0.2
D&O licence	3.60	0.7	4.49	1.7
Building permit fee	0.49	0.1	0.63	0.2
Entertainment	0.38	0.1	1.53	0.6
Fines/Penalties	0.35	0.1	0.56	0.2
Surcharges	0.21	0.0	0.00	0.0
Others	215.84	43.2	71.03	27.4
Total	499.36	100.0	259.10	100.0

arrear amount of D&O license fee, building permit fee, entertainment tax and fines and penalties. An arrear amount of ₹259 lakh per municipality is not a good indicator of the financial management of the municipalities.

Devolution of Funds: General Purpose, Maintenance and Development

The three categories of funds devolved to municipalities are general purpose, maintenance and development fund. The funds are transferred as per recommendation of 4th SFC during the period covered in the study.

GPF is primarily meant for meeting expenditure for the execution of the mandatory functions of municipalities as stipulated in the KMA, 1994, and other basic functions. Most of the mandatory functions are the traditional civic functions like collection and disposal of solid waste, disposal of liquid waste, regulation of slaughtering of animals, street lighting, establishment of burial and burning grounds, provision of parking spaces for vehicles, construction of waiting sheds, provision of public toilet facilities, control of stray dogs population, provision of facilities in slum areas, etc. However, the fund shall be used for the following purposes also: (a) to cover the deficit in own funds for meeting administrative, establishment, operating and other items of expenditure; (b) to meet the items of recurring expenditure of the TIs which were met from the non-road maintenance fund. Table 6.7 gives the amount received as GPF.

Maintenance fund is meant for meeting the maintenance expenditure of the assets of municipalities and assets of TIs. Maintenance comprises of repairs and replacements of spare items plus other requirements needed to retain an asset in working condition. Two categories of maintenance funds given are (a) for road and (b) for non-road assets. Repair and maintenance of all types of roads of the urban LGs including roads constructed under MP and Member of Legislative Assembly (MLA) Fund, PMGSY, flood relief, etc., is covered under maintenance fund. The amount of maintenance fund received per municipality for road is given in Table 6.7.

Table 6.7 *Amount Received per Municipality through Devolution: Amount, Composition and Growth Rate*

Category of Fund	2011–2012 (₹ in Lakh)	2012–2013 (₹ in Lakh)	2013–2014 (₹ in Lakh)	2014–2015 (₹ in Lakh)	2014–2015 Composition (%)
General Purpose	156.22	126.74	155.90	131.56	11.7
Development (excluding World Bank loan and 13th UFC Grant)	326.55	333.11	461.53	421.68	37.6
Maintenance (road)	95.13	112.31	145.71	142.67	12.7
Maintenance (non-road)	72.15	88.32	120.60	126.23	11.3
World Bank loan	30.24	57.88	27.09	72.08	6.4
13th UFC grant	104.30	170.14	180.36	226.33	20.2
Total	**784.59**	**888.50**	**1,091.18**	**1,120.56**	**100.0**
Growth rate (%)		13.2	22.8	2.7	

Maintenance fund for non-road assets is another item of devolved funds (Table 6.7). It is used for repair and maintenance of all non-road assets including assets of TIs, hospital buildings, furniture, machineries and equipment, toilets, computers and allied equipment including annual maintenance contract (AMC), and all other non-road assets including own assets. Maintenance of school buildings, including roof changing of thatched buildings/semi-permanent buildings, electrical wiring/rewiring, plumbing works, replacement/repair of existing plumbing items, construction of compound wall, repair, maintenance and improvement of school kitchen, drinking water and sanitation. The fund may be also used for payment of electricity charges, water charges, purchase of furniture for schools, purchase of medicines, hospital equipment, computers, computer accessories, consumables, medicines, machineries, etc.

Development fund is meant to finance annual development plans of municipalities for the local-level development. The municipalities have freedom to formulate and execute annual plan consisting of a number of projects and schemes for local development, subject to the overall plan guidelines of the state government. The fund consists of a share of the state plan funded from state resources and borrowing, the World Bank loan and 13th UFC grant (Table 6.7). Among the three items of devolved funds, development fund accounts for the largest share (38%).

Centrally Sponsored Schemes and Social Welfare Schemes

The municipalities execute agency functions such as implementation of CSS of the Union Government and welfare pension schemes of the state government. The major items of CSS receipts are Kudumbashree, MP Fund, flood relief, ICDS and SGSY/SJSRY. The total amount received per municipality ranged between ₹65 lakh and ₹178 lakh during a period of four years (Table 6.8).

The state government had transferred the functions of delivery of social welfare pensions to the municipalities. Here, the funds are given by the state government and the role of municipalities is to

Table 6.8 *CSS Receipts per Municipality: Amount, Composition and Growth Rate*

Item	2011– 2012 (₹ in Lakh)	2012– 2013 (₹ in Lakh)	2013– 2014 (₹ in Lakh)	2014– 2015 (₹ in Lakh)	2014–2015 Composition (%)
Flood relief	5.90	6.00	5.14	3.92	2.4
ICDS	0.75	3.41	2.98	2.27	1.4
Kudumbashree	6.47	4.79	10.30	14.00	8.5
MP fund	7.14	7.07	17.19	6.02	3.7
NREGS	0.36	2.09	9.70	2.08	1.3
SSA	2.63	0.79	0.80	0.00	0.0
Total sanitation	1.01	3.31	2.49	1.27	0.8
SGSY/SJSRY	1.10	0.88	4.19	3.64	2.2
Others	152.68	36.83	129.27	130.61	79.7
Total	**178.03**	**65.17**	**182.05**	**163.82**	**100**
Growth rate (%)		–63.4	179.4	–10.0	

distribute the pensions periodically to actual beneficiaries directly or through postal transfer or through bank accounts. Table 6.9 presents the amount of welfare pension receipts per municipality for a period of four years. Though a number of CSS schemes and social welfare pensions were transferred to the municipalities, adequate additional staff was not given to them.

GROWTH AND STRUCTURE OF EXPENDITURE

The expenditure is classified into eight items, namely administration, establishment, annual plan, maintenance, O&M, miscellaneous, CSS and welfare pension. The average total expenditure per municipality ranged between ₹1,988 lakh and ₹2,628 lakh during the period 2011–2012 and 2014–2015 (Table 6.10). An examination of the

Table 6.9 *Welfare Pension Receipts per Municipality: Amount, Composition and Growth Rate*

Welfare Pension	2011– 2012 (₹ in Lakh)	2012– 2013 (₹ in Lakh)	2013– 2014 (₹ in Lakh)	2014– 2015 (₹ in Lakh)	2014–2015 Composition (%)
Agricultural workers	34.89	35.44	34.34	34.04	11.5
Financial help for widow's daughters marriage	1.42	1.27	2.03	3.14	1.1
Destitute/Widow	4.49	82.56	101.79	104.73	35.3
Disabled	14.96	25.11	34.45	33.29	11.2
Old age	14.29	26.77	22.71	104.64	35.3
Unmarried women aged above 50	3.10	6.08	7.95	7.59	2.6
Production incentive to paddy growers	0.07	0.31	0.04	0.12	0.0
Unemployment allowance	6.75	6.49	3.89	6.33	2.1
Others	5.67	4.50	7.30	2.87	0.9
Total	**122.65**	**188.54**	**214.49**	**296.76**	**100**
Growth rate (%)		**53.7**	**13.8**	**38.4**	

Table 6.10 *Total Expenditure per Municipality: Amount, Composition and Growth*

Item of Expenditure	2011–2012	2012–2013	2013–2014	2014–2015
	₹ in Lakh			
Administration	59.68	102.29	144.12	58.18
CSS	187.65	73.73	168.64	160.87
Plan	803.48	618.70	1,021.02	889.26
Establishment	392.77	417.04	493.34	469.59
Maintenance	134.51	158.32	283.28	276.37
Miscellaneous	56.40	174.32	165.01	57.46
O&M	230.29	165.43	141.66	99.73
Welfare pension	123.05	188.39	211.17	294.64
Total	**1,987.83**	**1,898.22**	**2,628.25**	**2,306.09**
	Composition (%)			
Administration	3.0	5.4	5.5	2.5
CSS	9.4	3.9	6.4	7.0
Decentralized plan programme	40.4	32.6	38.8	38.6
Establishment	19.8	22.0	18.8	20.4
Maintenance	6.8	8.3	10.8	12.0
Miscellaneous	2.8	9.2	6.3	2.5
O&M	11.6	8.7	5.4	4.3
Welfare pension	6.2	9.9	8.0	12.8
Total	**100.0**	**100.0**	**100.0**	**100.0**
	Growth (%)			
Administration		71.4	40.9	−59.6
CSS		−60.7	128.7	−4.6
Decentralized plan programme		−23.0	65.0	−12.9
Establishment		6.2	18.3	−4.8
Maintenance		17.7	78.9	−2.4
Miscellaneous		209.1	−5.3	−65.2
O&M		−28.2	−14.4	−29.6
Welfare pension		53.1	12.1	39.5
Total		**−4.5**	**38.5**	**−12.3**

structure of expenditure indicates the following. Annual plan accounts for the single largest share of expenditure. It ranged between 33 and 40 per cent of the total expenditure. Establishment expenditure is the second major item of expenditure ranging between 19 and 22 per cent of the total expenditure. Welfare pension is the third major item of expenditure and accounts for 6 to 13 per cent of the total expenditure. Maintenance expenditure inclusive of road and non-road accounted for the fourth major item of expenditure. Expenditure on CSS, O&M, administration and miscellaneous are the other items of expenditure. Thus, an important aspect of the total expenditure was the spending of about 39 per cent on annual plans (Table 6.10).

Administration and Establishment

An attempt is made to examine the major individual items of administrative expenditure consisting of office expenses, expenses related to TIs, expenses connected with conduct of the meeting of ward sabha, electricity charges of office buildings, rents paid for the buildings hired and other items. Table 6.11 presents administrative expenses

Table 6.11 *Administrative Expenditure per Municipality: Amount, Composition and Growth Rate*

Item of Expenditure	2011–2012 (₹ in Lakh)	2012–2013 (₹ in Lakh)	2013–2014 (₹ in Lakh)	2014–2015 (₹ in Lakh)	2014–2015 Composition (%)
Office expenses	24.33	24.80	18.63	16.12	27.7
Expenses relating to transferred institutions	8.03	24.08	55.80	24.39	41.9
Ward sabha expenses	0.05	0.46	0.05	0.05	0.1
Office electricity charges	3.07	1.85	4.93	1.54	2.6
Rent on buildings	0.61	0.33	1.14	0.89	1.5
TA of chairperson, etc.	0.25	0.30	0.18	2.93	5.0
Other items	23.34	50.47	63.38	12.27	21.1
Total	59.68	102.29	144.12	58.19	100.0
Growth rate (%)		71.4	0.41	−59.6	

per municipality for a period of four years. Recurring expenditure of TIs is the largest item of expenditure in 2014–2015.

Establishment expenditure is another item related to the payments given to staff, chairperson and elected members of municipality, etc. The items coming under this category are salary, wages, TAs, pension contribution of staff, honorarium and TA paid to chairperson and elected members of the municipality, etc. Table 6.12 gives establishment expenditure per municipality for a period of four years. Salaries of permanent staff, wages of temporary staff and pension contribution of staff accounts for about 93 per cent of the total establishment expenditure.

Annual Plan Expenditure

Municipalities allot plan funds to various sectors based on the plan formulation guidelines of the state government. The sector-wise division of the plan expenditure are infrastructure, production, service and others not included in the sector classification. The annual plan expenditure includes the spill-over expenditure of the plan projects

Table 6.12 *Establishment Expenditure per Municipality: Amount, Composition and Growth Rate*

Item	2011–2012 (₹ in Lakh)	2012–2013 (₹ in Lakh)	2013–2014 (₹ in Lakh)	2014–2015 (₹ in Lakh)	2014–2015 Composition (%)
Salary	277.29	298.11	333.89	358.64	76.4
Wages	23.21	27.01	51.07	32.12	6.8
Honorarium and sitting fees of chairperson, etc.	14.89	15.05	19.82	16.85	3.6
Pension contribution	43.58	47.05	58.03	44.31	9.4
TA of employees, other allowances	0.59	0.67	0.63	0.63	0.1
Other expenditure	33.21	29.14	29.90	17.04	3.6
Total	**392.77**	**417.04**	**493.34**	**469.59**	**100.0**
Growth rate (%)		**6.2**	**18.3**	**−4.8**	

and schemes of the previous year. From Table 6.13, we can make the following inferences about the trend, composition and pattern of plan expenditure. A positive aspect was the growth in the share of expenditure on infrastructure sector. But a negative aspect was the low share or low priority given to productive sector. Other negative aspects are allotment of about 43 per cent of plan expenditure for service sector and steep decline in expenditure on projects not included in sector classification was another limitation. Poor utilization of plan outlay is a serious issue of plan performance.

Maintenance Expenditure

Maintenance funds are given to municipalities for maintaining the assets of their own and TIs. The fund is used for two purposes, namely maintenance of road assets and non-road assets. After meeting maintenance needs, the surplus fund can be used for construction of new roads and upgradation of roads. An analysis of the composition of maintenance fund shows that 53 to 63 per cent of the fund was spent for maintenance of the roads belonging to municipalities (Table 6.14).

The expenditure on maintenance of non-road assets like own buildings of municipalities and buildings of TIs like schools, hospitals,

Table 6.13 *Expenditure on Decentralized Plan per Municipality: Amount, Composition and Growth*

Sector	2011–2012 (₹ in Lakh)	2012–2013 (₹ in Lakh)	2013–2014 (₹ in Lakh)	2014–2015 (₹ in Lakh)	2014–2015 Composition (%)
Infrastructure	278.51	270.49	499.46	428.40	48.2
Production	70.91	40.77	49.43	68.70	7.7
Projects not included in sector division	166.64	4.98	6.24	7.80	0.9
Service	287.41	302.45	465.89	384.35	43.2
Total	803.48	618.70	1021.02	889.26	100.0
Growth rate (%)		–23.0	65.0	–12.9	

Table 6.14 *Maintenance Expenditure per Municipality: Amount, Composition and Growth*

Category	2011– 2012 (₹ in Lakh)	2012– 2013 (₹ in Lakh)	2013– 2014 (₹ in Lakh)	2014– 2015 (₹ in Lakh)	2014–2015 Composition (%)
Non-road assets	49.28	61.72	97.85	129.06	46.7
Road assets	85.24	96.60	185.43	147.31	53.3
Total	134.51	158.32	283.28	276.37	100.0
Growth rate (%)		17.7	78.9	–2.4	

veterinary centres, krishi bhavans, etc., accounts for 35 to 47 per cent of the fund. A notable aspect was the substantial increase in the share of maintenance expenditure during the year 2014–2015 (Table 6.14).

Operation and Maintenance, and Miscellaneous Expenditure

The O&M expenditure includes electricity charges for street lights, water charges for street taps, fuel expenses of vehicles, sanitation expenses and other repair and maintenance expenses. Table 6.15 gives O&M expenditure per municipality for a period of four years. A composition of the expenditure shows that nearly 44 per cent of it was spent as electricity charges for street lighting. The amount was paid to Kerala State Electricity Board which provides electricity for street lights in the electric posts owned and maintained by the Board. Another 31 per cent was spent for repairs and maintenance of other assets. Eight per cent of O&M expenditure was spent as water charges for street taps provided by Kerala Water Authority, which supplies drinking water in urban areas.

Miscellaneous expenditure includes items like depreciation, drought and flood relief, compensation from own fund, interest and finance charges, the amount written off, etc. Table 6.16 gives the miscellaneous items of expenditure for a period of four years. The major items of the expenditure of municipalities under these items are drought and flood relief, depreciation, the amount written off, compensation from own fund and interest charges.

Table 6.15 O&M Expenditure per Municipality: Amount, Composition and Growth

Item of Expenditure	2011–2012 (₹ in Lakh)	2012–2013 (₹ in Lakh)	2013–2014 (₹ in Lakh)	2014–2015 (₹ in Lakh)	2014–2015 Composition (%)
Repairs and maintenance of other assets (not included in plan)	149.13	73.83	53.88	31.22	31.3
Electricity charges for street lights	23.43	32.27	34.01	43.56	43.7
Water charges for street taps	24.46	33.49	14.79	8.34	8.4
Repairs and maintenance of buildings (not included in plan)	16.72	7.41	9.47	1.90	1.9
Diesel, petrol, gas and lubricants for vehicle	6.51	6.21	7.44	6.27	6.3
Sanitation	4.30	6.19	3.70	2.13	2.1
Other items	5.75	6.02	18.38	6.30	6.3
Total	**230.29**	**165.43**	**141.66**	**99.73**	**100.0**
Growth rate (%)		**−28.2**	**−14.4**	**−29.6**	

Table 6.16 Miscellaneous Expenditure per Municipality: Amount, Composition and Growth

Item	2011–2012 (₹ in Lakh)	2012–2013 (₹ in Lakh)	2013–2014 (₹ in Lakh)	2014–2015 (₹ in Lakh)	2014–2015 Composition (%)
Depreciation	27.99	47.35	115.13	13.74	8.5
Drought and flood relief	1.69	88.03	14.51	13.91	8.6
Grants, contributions and compensation from own fund	12.85	3.45	9.11	8.83	5.5
Interest and finance charges	11.64	12.10	13.93	6.86	4.3
Provisions and write-off	20.06	9.18	20.88	12.68	7.9
Others	83.68	328.00	288.47	104.85	65.2
Total	**157.91**	**488.10**	**462.03**	**160.88**	**100**
Growth rate (%)		**209.1**	**−5.3**	**−65.2**	

Welfare Pensions

The municipalities have been implementing a number of social welfare schemes of the state government. Here, the funds are given by the state government and the function of municipalities is to distribute it to the beneficiaries. Table 6.17 gives the amount of welfare pension distributed by the municipalities for a period of four years. There had been a steady increase in total amount dispersed. Widow pension ranked first in terms of the amount dispersed and accounts for 35.5 per cent of the total amount in 2014–2015. Old-age pension is the second largest item accounting for 35.2 per cent of the total amount disbursed. Agricultural workers pension and disabled pension account for 23 per cent of the total. Thus, of the total amount, 94 per cent was spent for the aforementioned four items of pension.

The social welfare pension schemes were distributed by the government departments directly to the beneficiaries prior to 1996. The schemes having large number of beneficiaries were transferred to municipalities between 1996 and 2001 resulting in substantial increase in the administrative work of urban LGs. The work involves updating the list of pensioners, deletion and addition of beneficiaries, sending money orders, remitting the amount in bank accounts of beneficiaries, etc. The entire work was done manually till recently. The available evidence suggests that the transfer of pension distribution without corresponding changes in administration and staff has adversely affected the functioning of the municipalities.

Centrally Sponsored Scheme

Table 6.18 gives the item-wise expenditure of CSS for a period of four years implemented by the municipalities. The total expenditure on CSS per municipality ranged between ₹206 lakh and ₹525 lakh. Among the CSS, the major items are Kudumbashree, MP Fund, SGSRY, SJSRY and total sanitation. The other items which accounted for less than 1.5 per cent of the total CSS expenditure are Basic Services to Urban Poor (BSUP), flood relief, ICDS, NREGS, National Rural Health Mission (NRHM) and SSA. A review of the trends in total expenditure shows that there had been a negative growth in the years 2013–2014 and 2014–2015.

Table 6.17 *Welfare Pension Expenditure per Municipality: Amount, Composition and Growth*

Welfare Pension	2011–2012 (₹ in Lakh)	2012–2013 (₹ in Lakh)	2013–2014 (₹ in Lakh)	2014–2015 (₹ in Lakh)	2014–2015 Composition (%)
Agricultural workers	104.00	102.77	95.70	95.34	11.6
Financial help for widow's daughters marriage	4.21	3.57	5.68	7.95	1.0
Destitute/Widow	119.50	230.69	284.60	293.08	35.5
Disabled	42.87	70.21	96.06	93.15	11.3
Old age	40.18	74.75	63.46	290.61	35.2
Unmarried women aged above 50	8.71	16.96	22.11	21.25	2.6
Production incentive to paddy growers	0.78	0.93	0.80	0.46	0.0
Unemployment allowance	18.87	18.15	11.98	17.38	2.1
Other pensions/assistance	5.42	9.45	10.89	5.76	0.7
Total	**344.53**	**527.48**	**591.28**	**824.98**	**100**
Growth rate (%)		**53.1**	**12.1**	**39.5**	

Table 6.18 Expenditure on CSS per Municipality: Amount, Composition and Growth

Item	2011–2012 (₹ in Lakh)	2012–2013 (₹ in Lakh)	2013–2014 (₹ in Lakh)	2014–2015 (₹ in Lakh)	2014–2015 Composition (%)
BSUP/IHSDP	85.19	17.71	61.29	5.09	1.1
Flood relief	6.83	25.03	16.84	6.59	1.5
ICDS	9.58	12.05	15.45	6.03	1.3
Kudumbashree	7.92	23.78	21.17	20.86	4.6
MP Fund	19.81	16.02	54.67	17.84	4.0
NREGS	0.64	1.81	3.22	1.85	0.4
NRHM/NUHM	2.16	9.18	8.84	3.04	0.7
SGRY	0.95	1.71	1.77	17.22	3.8
SGSY/SJSRY	2.55	1.78	16.35	14.38	3.2
SSA	8.49	9.48	8.73	3.00	0.7
Total sanitation	4.12	19.92	2.01	12.42	2.8
Other items	377.18	67.97	261.86	342.11	75.9
Total	**525.43**	**206.45**	**472.19**	**450.43**	**100**
Growth rate (%)		−60.7	128.7	−4.6	

Pension Payment Problem of Retired Staff

A serious problem faced by municipalities is the payment of monthly pension and other retirement benefits to retired staff. The staff of the GPs, BPs and DPs are treated at par with the state government staff in the matter of recruitment and payment of pensions. The retirement benefits and monthly pensions are paid by the state government and are similar to that of the staff belonging to government departments. But in the case of municipalities and MCs, the temporary staff is appointed by them and permanent staff through Kerala Public Service Commission. And the responsibility to pay the retirement benefits and pensions is vested with the municipalities and MCs. Though an arrangement was made between the state government and urban LGs to pay the pension based on the contribution from the two sides, the system has not been working satisfactorily. Due to this, municipalities are forced to pay pensions and retirement benefits by diverting other funds resulting in fiscal crisis. The data collected from the 13 sample municipalities revealed that the total number of pensioners was 1,259 and the total retirement benefits and monthly pension paid to the pensioners was ₹1,691 lakh in 2013–2014 (Table 6.19).

The pension issue became very complex and reached an unmanageable level due to the following reasons: (a) a municipality has to pay pension benefits not only to the staff retiring from it but also to the staff who retired from other municipalities. Those who retire from other municipalities have the freedom to opt for pension from any of the municipalities in Kerala of their choice; (b) the Director of Urban Affairs, who is responsible for giving funds for the payment of pensions, fails to give funds to the municipalities in time mainly due to inadequate budgetary provisions; (c) due to this, the municipalities are forced to divert their own fund and GPF for paying pensions and other retirement benefits; (d) some of the municipalities are not remitting the pension contribution of staff to the government as they have to get huge amount of pension dues from the Director of Urban Affairs; (e) among the 13 municipalities that supplied data, only 4 reported that they remitted the pension contribution for the year 2014–2015; (f) the municipalities told us that their demand was that the government should take over the responsibility of pension commitment and

Table 6.19 *Pension Payments to Retired Staff in 2013–2014*

Sl No.	Name of Sample Municipalities	Number of Pensioners	Pension and Retirement Benefit Paid (₹ in Lakh)
1	Nedumangad	15	43.25
2	Thiruvalla	85	136.74
3	Alappuzha	282	354.93
4	Kottayam	364	554.03
5	Thodupuzha	52	71.51
6	North Paravur	52	0.00
7	Kunnamkulam	74	82.37
8	Shoranur	51	63.71
9	Manjeri	34	42.00
10	Vatakara	140	205.18
11	Kalpetta	17	19.64
12	Payyanur	23	45.56
13	Kasaragod	70	72.27
	Total	**1,259**	**1,691.19**

disbursement. The 5th SFC which examined the issue gave a few recommendations to solve the issue of timely payment of pension dues from the government and timely payment of pension contribution by the urban LGs.

CONCLUSION

Though additional expenditure responsibilities are assigned to municipalities through the enactment of KMA, 1994, they were not given new tax or non-tax items or to effect periodical revision of its rates. While tax and non-tax items accounted for 26 per cent, share of transferred funds was 38 per cent, welfare pensions and CSS were 21 per cent of the total revenue receipts in 2014–2015. Though there is considerable scope for increasing their tax and non-tax revenue, through periodical revision, they could not implement it due to lack of powers. A review of the structure of expenditure shows that annual plan accounts the large share followed by establishment, maintenance, welfare pensions and CSS.

The issue of payment of retirement benefits and pensions to retired municipal staff has emerged as a serious fiscal problem of the municipalities. This is mainly due to the fact that the arrangement of pension payment by contributing a share by the state government (Director of Urban Affairs) and other share by the municipalities have collapsed. Entrusting additional agency functions such as distribution of social welfare pension and implementation of CSS have adversely affected the execution of their civic functions like waste disposal, waste water disposal, containing stray dog menace, running slaughter houses, public toilets, etc.

State Finance Commissions in Kerala

A Review

The important preconditions required for a sound fiscal decentralization system of an LG are the following: (a) clear assignment of functions and expenditure responsibilities; (b) allocation of own source revenue and powers to levy, collect and revise taxes, fees, user charges, etc., assigned to the LGs; (c) unconditional and formula-driven intergovernmental transfers to cover the gap in resources between own resources and expenditure; and (d) powers to borrow funds for meeting current and capital items of expenditure. Among them, the core one is intergovernmental fiscal transfers. The intergovernmental fiscal transfers refers to the transfer of finances from the higher level of governments (centre or state) to lower government levels (LGs). In general, the revenue assignment never matches the expenditure needs, so intergovernmental fiscal transfers are often necessary to assure revenue adequacy. It ensures bridging the vertical fiscal gap, improve horizontal fiscal balance, fund national priorities, compensate for spillovers or externalities, etc. The total amount of transfers may be determined in three ways: (a) rule-based fixed percentage share of dedicated revenues, (b) ad hoc (normally as part of annual budget decision) and (c) as a proportion of approved specific local expenditures to be reimbursed. Of the three, the rule-based transfer system brings greater stability and predictability, and hence promotes good planning and efficient service delivery effort.

In the Indian federal set-up, the intergovernmental fiscal transfers are done by the institutions, namely UFC (from centre to state) and SFCs (from state to LGs). In this context, we examine the role of SFCs in fiscal decentralization of Kerala. The aspects examined are constitution of SFCs, status of implementations of SFC reports and devolution recommendations.

CONSTITUTION OF SFCS AND STATUS OF IMPLEMENTATION OF REPORTS

Kerala is a pioneer state in India in terms of effecting fiscal decentralization of LGs by constituting SFCs. The state government had constituted five SFCs to review the financial position of LGs, recommend devolution of state taxes, distribution of grants-in-aid and measures to strengthen the financial position of the LGs. The Government of Kerala (GoK) constituted the 1st SFC under clause 1 of Article 243(I) of the Constitution of India and Section 186 of the KPRA, 1994, with Shri P. M. Abraham as chairman. Table 7.1 gives the date of constitution, names of chairman and members of the SFCs.

The Commission submitted its reports to the governor of Kerala on 29 February 1996 and the Action Taken Report was presented in the Kerala Legislative Assembly on 13 March 1997. Table 7.2 presents date of submission of SFC reports, date of presentation of the reports

Table 7.1 *Chairman and Members of SFCs in Kerala*

Name of the Commission	Date of Constitution of the Commission	Chairman of the Commissions	Members of the Commission
1st SFC	23 April 1994	Shri P. M. Abraham	Shri K. Mohandas Shri K. A. Ommer
2nd SFC	23 June 1999	Dr Prabhat Patnaik	Dr K. M. Abraham Shri S. M. Vijayanand
3rd SFC	20 September 2004	Shri K. V. Rabindran Nair	Shri V. S. Senthil Shri P. Kamalkutty
4th SFC	19 September 2009	Professor M. A. Oommen	Shri S. M. Vijayanand Smt Ishita Roy
5th SFC	17 December 2014	Professor B. A. Prakash	Shri James Varghese Dr V. K. Baby

Source: Government of Kerala (2015, 2016).

Table 7.2 *Date of Submission and Presentation of SFC Reports in Legislative Assembly*

Name of Commission	Date of Submission of Report	Date of Presentation in Legislative Assembly	Award Period
1st SFC	29 February 1996	13 March 1997	1996–1997 to 2000–2001
2nd SFC	8 January 2001	7 January 2004	2001–2002 to 2005–2006
3rd SFC	23 November 2005	16 February 2006	2006–2007 to 2010–2011
4th SFC	Part I: 22 January 2011 Part II: 31 March 2011	24 February 2011 22 March 2012	2011–2012 to 2015–2016
5th SFC	Part I: 19 December 2015 Part II: 11 March 2016	7 February 2018 7 February 2018	2016–2017 to 2020–2021

Source: Government of Kerala (2015, 2016).

along with Action Taken Report to the Kerala Legislative Assembly and award period of the SFCs.

Of the 69 recommendations of the Commission, the government accepted 63 recommendations (91%) but implemented 25 recommendations. Table 7.3 gives the total number of recommendations, number accepted and number implemented in case of the five SFCs. Though the state government was prompt in appointing the Commissions, the government had implemented only 36 per cent of the recommendations.

The government constituted the 2nd SFC on 23 June 1999 with Dr Prabhat Patnaik as the chairman. Though the 2nd SFC had submitted its report in January 2001, the Action Taken Report was presented in Kerala Legislative Assembly only after 3 years. Due to this, the state government delayed the implementations by 3 years. And the LGs in Kerala were denied their legitimate share of state taxes recommended by the Commission for three years from 2001–2002 to 2003–2004. The state government also implemented only about one-fourth of the total number of recommendations of the Commission.

Table 7.3 *Number of Recommendations Accepted and Rejected*

Name of Commission	Total Number of Recommendations	Number Accepted	Number Implemented	Number Accepted (% to Total)	Number Implemented (% to Total)
1st SFC	69	63	25	91.30	36.23
2nd SFC	49	43	13	87.76	26.53
3rd SFC	32	30	10	93.75	31.25
4th SFC	Part I: 46	21	18	45.65	39.13
	Part II: 105	87	7	82.86	6.67
	Total: 151	108	25	71.52	16.56
5th SFC	133	78	—	58.65	—

Source: Government of Kerala (2008, 2015, 2016).

The third SFC was constituted on 20 September 2004 with Shri K. V. Rabindran Nair as the chairman. The state government had taken prompt action on the report and the same was implemented from 2006–2007. Of the 32 recommendations of the Commission, 10 recommendations were implemented.

The 4th SFC was constituted on 19 September 2009 with Professor M. A. Oommen as chairman. The Commission submitted two parts of the reports on (a) issues on fiscal matters and (b) measures needed for proper institutionalization of the decentralization initiatives. Of the 46 recommendations relating to devolution, own resource mobilization and other fiscal issues in Part I of the report, 18 were implemented (39%). But with regard to the other 105 recommendations in Part II of the report, on asset management, financial management, institutionalization, recommendations to the Government of India, building database, DPC, only 7 were implemented. This means that all the recommendations in Part II of the report were not implemented except a few (Table 7.3). Table 7.4 gives the item-wise recommendations of the Commission accepted and referred to a committee.

It is interesting to note that 23 recommendations on own resource mobilization were referred to another committee. Even after 6 years, the so-called committee has not taken any action on the subject. Another disturbing aspect was that the government declared in the Action Taken Report presented in the Kerala Legislative Assembly that they had accepted most of the recommendations in Part II. This gives the impression that the government is going to implement it. But, in reality, the government has no intention to implement it. Of the 87 recommendations accepted in Part II, only 7 were implemented.

An interesting aspect is that the responsibility of processing the SFC recommendations and implementation is vested with the department of finance, a department having little role in the affairs of LGs. On the other hand, the Local Self Government Department (LSGD), which administers the affairs of the LGs, has little say in the implementation of the SFC recommendations. This is also one of the reasons for non-implementation of the recommendations on items other than devolution.

Table 7.4 *4th SFC Number of Recommendations Accepted and Others*

Sl No	Item	Total Number of Recommendations	Number Accepted	Number Accepted with Modification	Referred to a Committee	% of Accepted to Total
		Part I of the Report				
1	Devolution	20	20	–	–	100
2	Own revenue mobilization	23	–	–	23	–
3	Borrowing	1	–	–	1	–
4	Streamlining accounts	1	1	–	–	100
5	Review of previous SFCs recommendations	1	–	–	1	–
	Subtotal	**46**	**21**	**–**	**25**	**45.65**
		Part II of the Report				
6	Asset management	12	8	4	–	66.67
7	Financial management	17	15	2	–	88.24
8	Good practices	6	6	–	–	100
9	Institutionalization	58	47	3	8	81.03
10	Recommendations to the Government of India	3	2	–	1	66.67
11	Building database	3	3	–	–	100
12	CSS	1	1	–	–	100
13	DPC	5	5	–	–	100
	Subtotal	**105**	**87**	**9**	**9**	**82.86**
	Grand total	**151**	**108**	**9**	**9**	**71.52**

Source: Government of Kerala (2011, 2012).

From the earlier review, we can conclude as follows. The successive governments in Kerala took steps to constitute SFCs in a time-bound manner. They wanted to give an impression that they are serious about SFCs and going to implement their recommendations. But, in practice, they implemented only a few recommendations on devolution and rejected almost all other recommendations on one pretext or another. The percentage of recommendations implemented during the first four SFCs ranged between 17 and 39 per cent of the total.

DEVOLUTION RECOMMENDATIONS OF SFCS

Recommendations of 1st SFC

The major recommendations of the Commission on devolution are presented in the section. For devolving plan funds, the Commission used the following criteria. For devolution of plan funds for local bodies, the following criteria with weightage was recommended. For urban local bodies, 75 per cent weightage was given to population based on 1991 Census, 10 per cent for SC/ST population and 15 per cent for total workers excluding workers in industry and services outside household industry. For rural local bodies, 75 per cent weightage was given for population, 10 per cent for SC/ST population, 10 per cent for workers excluding industry and services outside household industry and 10 per cent for the share of agricultural workers to total workers. The recommendations of the Commission relating to non-plan grants are given as follows: (a) it should be left to the local bodies to decide on the application of the non-plan grants according to their own priority and perception of their needs; (b) non-statutory non-plan grants may be fixed at 1 per cent of the state revenue and may be distributed between urban and rural local bodies in proportion to their population; (c) the constitution of state-level fund for GPs and municipal councils called the rural pool and urban pool, respectively, and recommended a criterion for distribution of the funds. It was also recommended composite criteria which includes population as well as other relevant factors; (d) PRI should be provided with funds for maintenance of assets at prescribed norms and (e) the additional expenditure arising from the provisions of the KPRA, 1994, in respect of the two new tiers, namely the DP and BP may be provided by grant-in-aid by the government.

Recommendations of 2nd SFC

The Commission has recommended three items of funds to local self-government institutions (LSGIs), namely plan fund, maintenance fund and GPF.

Plan Fund

Government may devolve to the LSGIs, plan funds (excluding state-sponsored schemes) not less than one-third of the annual size of the state plan as fixed by the Planning Commission. This fund is to be used by LSGIs for planning and implementing locally relevant projects. The sectoral ceilings, if any, within this grant may be fixed by the government from time to time.

Maintenance Fund

Five and a half per cent of the annual own tax revenue of the state government may be devolved to the LSGIs as grant-in-aid for maintenance of assets under the control of the LSGIs including the transferred assets. This percentage may be determined on the figures certified by the accountant general, which normally relates to the financial year two years before the budget year. All expenses related to running of institutions except wages, supply of medicines to health institutions, educational concessions/scholarships to students, supply of books, equipment and consumables to schools and conducting noon-feeding in schools, shall be borne by the LSGIs. This should include payment of rents, repair of equipment including vehicles, and meeting of telephone charges and vehicle operating expenses.

General Purpose Grant

Three and a half per cent of the own tax revenue of the state government based on the figures certified by the accountant general could be devolved to LSGIs as General Purpose Grant in lieu of assigned taxes, shared taxes and various statutory and non-statutory grants-in-aid, both specific and general purpose. This grant-in-aid would subsume under it basic tax grant, surcharge on stamp duty, vehicle tax compensation, rural pool grants, the specific purpose and general purpose grants to urban local bodies and all other non-plan grants-in-aid devolved to LSGIs from the LSGD.

RECOMMENDATIONS OF 3RD SFC

The 3rd SFC wanted to maintain broadly the same level (dimensionally) of devolution as recommended by the 2nd SFC. The Commission pointed out that the constitutional amendment changed the limited role as well as the status of local bodies drastically. More services and institutions were transferred, making them another level of governance, taking over the load of a part of the functions of the state government. The function of formulating and implementing development plans were also assigned to the LSGs. The LSGs in Kerala were now entitled to receive a share of state government taxes for three purposes: (a) to augment their own resources to meet their traditional functions, (b) to maintain the services and institutions transferred to them and (c) to extend and develop those services and institutions.

Norms of Devolution

The norms of the devolution are as follows: (a) the 3rd SFC recommended an amount of around 25 per cent of the total state tax revenue of the year 2003–2004 for transferring to LSGs during the year 2006–2007. Thus, for the base year devolution, the Commission used $t-3$ method which is based on SOTR received three years back. During each of the four subsequent years, the amount was derived by applying annual growth of 10 per cent; (b) the Commission accepted the same share of state taxes recommended by the 2nd SFC for transfer to LSGs; (c) the Commission recommended 3.5 per cent of the share of state taxes for meeting traditional functions expenditure; (d) for meeting maintenance expenditure, the Commission recommended a share of 5.5 per cent of share of state taxes and (e) the Commission recommended the award specifying the amount of money to be devolved to each LG for each year for the award period of 5 years.

Recommendations of 4th SFC

The Commission recommended a vertical transfer system with five components, namely (a) GPF, (b) support for the fiscally weak LGs, (c) maintenance fund, (d) development fund and (e) special grants (SGs) for deprived GPs.

General Purpose Fund

The Commission has recommended that the status quo ante be restored and the LGs be given 3.5 per cent of SOTR using the $t-2$ method, that is, for devolution in a particular year, the tax collection figures of two years back is taken. This means that devolution of resources is based on SOTR received two years back.

The GPF may be divided among GPs, municipalities and corporations in the ratio 75.93:10.02:14.05, after setting apart ₹125 lakh per DP and ₹15 lakh per BP. The gap fund (GF) may be deducted from the shares of GPs and the remaining amount distributed as per population.

Support for Fiscally Weak LGs

There were several GPs which were not able to meet their establishment costs and obligatory expenses (for which maintenance or development funds cannot be used) with their own revenues plus GPF. A GF was allotted to eligible GPs by the government after getting certified figures of the gap in the previous year specially prepared by the Director of Local Fund Audit and the distribution was to be made proportionate to the gap. An amount of ₹25 crore was set apart from the GPF available to GPs.

Maintenance Fund

The Commission has recommended 4.5 to 5.5 per cent of the SOTR calculated using $t-2$ method to be transferred as maintenance fund.

The percentage share of SOTR for the award period of the 4th SFC is given in Table 7.5.

The Commission has recommended to earmark two-thirds of the maintenance fund for road maintenance and the remaining one-third for non-road maintenance.

Development Fund

The Commission recommended an allocation of 25 per cent of the proposed plan size in 2011–2012 and thereafter increase it in relation to the plan size assumed by SFC based on the past trends. Table 7.6 gives the share of the assumed plan size and proposed allocation of the Commission. The Commission stipulated that minimum plan outlay should not be less than 25 per cent of the plan size under no

Table 7.5 *Maintenance Fund Award*

Year	(% Share of SOTR) (t – 2)
2011–2012	4.5
2012–2013	5.0
2013–2014	5.5
2014–2015	5.5
2015–2016	5.5

Source: Government of Kerala (2011).

Table 7.6 *Award of Development Fund*

Year	Share of the Assumed Plan Size (%)	Proposed Allocation (₹ in Crore)
2011–2012	25	2,750
2012–2013	27.5	3,388
2013–2014	28.5	3,933
2014–2015	29.5	4,559
2015–2016	30	5,193

Source: Government of Kerala (2011).

circumstances. The resources of the development fund consists of three items, namely resources from state non-plan, the World Bank loan and grants from 13th UFC.

Special Grants

The SGs given to Guruvayoor Municipality was enhanced from ₹14.64 lakh to ₹20 lakh and the special allocation given to GPs in Sabarimala region, namely Erumeli, Chittar, Ranni-Perunad, Vadasserikkara, Seethathode and Naranammoozhy was enhanced from ₹7.32 lakh to ₹10 lakh. Funds for providing awards for the best LGs would be continued to be met from the development fund. The Commission also recommended a SG of ₹25 lakh to each of the most vulnerable 16 GPs and a grant of ₹15 lakh to each of the vulnerable 58 GPs. And the total SG recommended was ₹12.70 crore.

Actual Transfer of Funds during the 4th SFC Period

In this section, we present actual transfer of funds as per the recommendation of the 4th SFC and its share in SOTR $(t-2)$ during the award period of four years. Here, the following data are used to find out resources from state own sources and UFC grants from the centre; (a) the amount of funds transferred under GPF and maintenance fund; (b) the three items of development fund such as share of SOTR, the World Bank loan and UFC grants and (c) data to estimate states own devolution and UFC grants from the central government. For finding the share of SOTR, we have used the data on SOTR $(t-2)$ basis, that is, tax revenue received two years back.

Table 7.7 gives the actual transfer of funds during the 4th SFC period of four years from the state own resources as well as from UFC grants from the central government.

The LGs in Kerala received 3.5 per cent of the SOTR on $t-2$ basis as GPF between 2011–2012 and 2014–2015. The share of maintenance fund ranged between 4.1 and 5.4 per cent of the SOTR. The share of development fund inclusive of the World Bank loan but exclusive of UFC grant ranged between 11.4 and 12.8 per cent of the SOTR. Thus,

Table 7.7 *Actual Transfer of Funds during 4th SFC Period (₹ in Crore)*

No.	Item	2011–2012	2012–2013	2013–2014	2014–2015
1	General Purpose Fund	622.23	757.89	900.15	1,052.68
2	Maintenance fund	712.94	1,039.45	1,386.94	1,542.45
3	Development fund (share of SOTR)	2,021.62	2,195.02	3,003.76	3,539.51
4	World Bank loan	140.00	284.25	270.01	319.40
5	Development fund (state's own) (3+4)	2,161.62	2,479.27	3,273.78	3,858.91
6	Total state's own devolution (1+2+5)	3,496.79	4,276.60	5,560.87	6,454.04
7	UFC grant	387.80	591.16	673.93	999.69
8	Total devolution (state's own + UFC grant)	3,884.59	4,867.76	6,234.79	7,453.74
	Gross tax revenue (t−2)	17,625	21,722	25,719	30,077

		As % of Gross Tax Revenue $(t-2)$				
1	General Purpose Fund	3.5	3.5	3.5	3.5
2	Maintenance fund	4.1	4.8	5.4	5.1
3	Development fund (share of SOTR)	11.5	10.1	11.9	11.8
4	World Bank loan	0.8	1.3	1.1	1.1
5	Development fund (state's own) (3+4)	12.3	11.4	12.8	12.8
6	Total state's own devolution (1+2+5)	19.8	19.7	21.6	21.5
7	UFC grant	2.2	2.7	2.6	3.3
8	Total devolution (state's own + UFC grant)	22.1	22.4	24.3	24.8

Source: Government of Kerala (2015).

total devolution of funds from state own sources as a share of SOTR and the World Bank loan accounted for 19.7 per cent to 21.6 per cent of the SOTR ($t-2$) during the four years.

An analysis of the LG-wise transfer of funds during the 4th SFC period of four years is given in Table 7.8. Of the total funds received by the LGs exclusive of UFC fund, major average share was received by the GPs (56.6%). DP is the category of LG which accounted for the second largest share of funds (14.4%). The other categories of LGs which rank third, fourth and fifth position are BPs, municipalities and MCs, respectively.

An attempt is also made to examine the fund-wise transfer excluding UFC grant during the year 2014–2015 (Table 7.9). Of the total GPF, the GPs received the largest share (70.7%) followed by the MCs and municipalities. In case of maintenance fund, the largest share was received by the GPs (59.2%), followed by the DPs and municipalities. Regarding development fund, the largest share was received by GPs (56.57%) followed by the DPs, BPs and municipalities. Thus, regarding all the three funds, the major share was received by the GPs.

CONCLUSIONS

Sound intergovernmental fiscal transfer through appropriate institutions is the cornerstone of fiscal decentralization. Kerala's experience of fiscal transfers through SFCs gives a mixed picture of merits as well as demerits. In other words, Kerala's achievement with regard to fiscal decentralization is partial.

Further, we give the merits and demerits. The merits are the following: (a) the successive governments in the state have been constituting SFCs at the expiry of every five years. Timely constitution of SFCs is a major achievement, (b) SFCs recommendations on fiscal devolution is based on clear fiscal norms; (c) a share of the state taxes and a share of the annual plan outlay are earmarked to the LGs for meeting their mandatory, maintenance and development functions. The major devolution recommendations of the successive SFCs are accepted except in the case of the 5th SFC; (d) the funds devolved are largely

Table 7.8 Transfer of Total Funds to LGs during the 4th SFC Period Excluding UFC Grant (₹ Crore)

LG	2011–2012	2012–2013	2013–2014	2014–2015	Four-Year Average
GP	1,936.91	2,499.33	3,126.04	3,649.00	2,802.82
BP	401.93	441.26	617.50	717.21	544.47
DP	503.14	572.65	839.58	935.92	712.82
Municipality	362.31	419.48	519.95	616.59	479.58
MC	292.49	343.88	457.80	535.32	407.38
Grand total	**3,496.79**	**4,276.60**	**5,560.87**	**6,454.04**	**4,947.07**
Composition (in %)					
GP	55.39	58.44	56.22	56.54	56.66
BP	11.49	10.32	11.10	11.11	11.01
DP	14.39	13.39	15.10	14.50	14.41
Municipality	10.36	9.81	9.35	9.55	9.69
MC	8.36	8.04	8.23	8.29	8.23
Grand total	**100**	**100**	**100**	**100**	**100**

Source: Government of Kerala (2015).

Table 7.9 Transfer of Funds to LGs in 2014–2015 Excluding UFC Grant (₹ in Crore)

LG	General Purpose Fund	Maintenance Fund	Development Fund	Total
GP	744.13	912.71	1,992.16	3,649.00
BP	42.56	53.66	620.99	717.21
DP	30.10	288.43	617.39	935.92
Municipality	98.20	166.92	351.48	616.59
MC	137.69	120.74	276.88	535.32
Total	**1,052.68**	**1,542.45**	**3,858.91**	**6,454.04**
Composition (in %)				
GP	70.7	59.2	51.6	56.5
BP	4.0	3.5	16.1	11.1
DP	2.9	18.7	16.0	14.5
Municipality	9.3	10.8	9.1	9.6
MC	13.1	7.8	7.2	8.3
Total	**100**	**100**	**100**	**100**

Source: Government of Kerala (2015).

sufficient to meet the expenditure responsibilities of urban and rural LGs; (e) the successive SFCs have been devolving funds on the basis of a category of funds (general purpose, maintenance and development) recommended by the 2nd SFC.

We may also examine the demerits: (a) deliberate and delayed implementation of SFC reports. Of the five SFCs, in the case of 2nd and 5th, the implementation was delayed by 3 years and 2 years, respectively; (b) implementation of a small share of recommendations. The percentage of recommendations implemented during the first four SFCs ranged between 17 and 39 per cent of the total; (c) the practice of non-implementation of recommendations other than devolution is a common practice. Of the 105 recommendations of the 4th SFC on asset management, financial management, institutionalization, building database, DPC etc., only 7 were implemented; (d) all the successive governments take a dual position, namely accepting a large number of recommendations in the Action Taken Report on the one hand and implementing only a few in actual practice on the other and (e) the processing of SFC recommendations in Kerala is done by the department of finance, bypassing the LSGD which is in charge of LGs.

Fifth State Finance Commission in Kerala

Devolution
Recommendations and
Status of Implementation

INTRODUCTION

In this chapter, we present terms of reference (ToR), approach to fiscal devolution, recommendations on vertical and horizontal devolution, actual transfer of funds of the 5th SFC and status of its implementation.

TERMS OF REFERENCE

The 5th SFC was constituted by the GoK with Professor B. A. Prakash as chairman and Shri James Varghese, IAS, and Shri Rabindrakumar Agarwal, IAS, as members on 17 December 2014. The ToR of the Commission were as follows. The Finance Commission shall review the financial position of the panchayats and the municipalities and make recommendations as to: (a) the principles which should govern: (i) the distribution between the state, panchayats and municipalities of the net proceeds of the taxes, duties, tolls and fees leviable by the state, and the allocation between the panchayats at all levels and the municipalities of their respective shares of such proceeds; (ii) the determination of the taxes, duties, tolls and fees which may be assigned to or appropriated by the panchayats and the municipalities;

(iii) the grants-in-aid to the panchayats and the municipalities from the Consolidated Fund of the State.

(b) The measures needed to strengthen the financial position of the panchayats and municipalities with special reference to the potential for LGs to raise funds from borrowing, improving the quality of upkeep of own assets and assets of TIs, rationalizing of taxes and revenues, achieving economy and efficiency in expenditure, providing incentives for higher own resource mobilization, etc., (c) the measures needed for the proper institutionalization of the decentralization initiatives in the state and (d) to revisit the recommendations of the first four SFCs, which were accepted but not operationalized and require changes.

DATA SOURCES

The 5th SFC conducted elaborate exercise to collect data and information on various aspects of LGs. In the sittings, conducted by the Commission in all districts, 139 LGs belonging to GPs, BPs, DPs, municipalities and MCs attended and presented their financial issues, problems and requirements and suggestions for devolution. The Commission has collected financial data through online-based detailed questionnaire from all the 1,200 LGs. Discussions were conducted with the heads of 15 government departments and institutions which are connected with the functioning of LGs. The Commission also held discussions with economists, policy experts and social scientists, office-bearers of GP, BP and DP associations, chamber of mayors and political parties.

APPROACH TO FISCAL DEVOLUTION

The 5th SFC felt that the approach to devolution followed by the previous SFCs require radical change due to the following reasons. First, the previous SFCs had used devolution of funds based on $(t-2)$ or $(t-3)$ method. Here, t represents the current year or year of devolution and $t-2$ indicates a year preceding two years. This means that the devolution of resources for the year 2018–2019 is done based on the proceeds of SOTR received during the year 2016–2017. Due to this practice, the LGs are denied their rightful share due to them based on SOTR of the year of devolution. Second, UFC is devolving resources from the centre to the states based on the estimated tax receipts of the year of devolution (t) and subsequently adjusting the amount with the actual receipts.

Third, the 3rd SFC had projected the resource availability of the state and the expenditure requirements of the LGs and recommended an annual devolution of resources for a period of five years for all LGs as well as for each LGs in advance. This recommendation was implemented successfully. Fourth, majority of the LGs that attended in the sittings of the Commission demanded that the SFC should give a recommendation specifying the amount of money to be given to each LG for each year of the award period of five years as in the case of the 3rd SFC. Fifth, in order to have a realistic projection of SOTR, the Commission attempted projection using 'baseline scenario', 'long-term trend-based method' and 'minimum buoyancy in SOTR' and compared them with the projection of the finance department of the state government. And based on this exercise, the Commission adopted 'minimum buoyancy in SOTR' method for projecting SOTR.

Sixth, the SFC has radically changed the norm of devolution to distribute development fund meant to finance annual plans. The approaches of the previous SFCs except the first and third SFCs were to fix a share of the annual plan size of Kerala as the share of the resources earmarked for development purposes of the LGs. The Commission was of the view that the approach has serious problems, namely (a) the constitutional articles, provisions in the KPRA, 1994, and the KMA, 1994, and the ToR of the Commission had not mandated the Commission to devolve the state resources based on the annual plan outlay of the state; (b) the estimated resources for state plan are not usually realized; (c) SFC has no authority to fix the plan outlay of the state, which consists of a number of items or components; (d) the mandate given by the earlier Acts and ToR was to share the net proceeds of tax resources of the state. In this context, the Commission recommended a share of the net proceeds of SOTR as calculated on (t) basis as the development fund.

Recommendation on Devolution

Taking into consideration the earlier aspects, the 5th SFC presented the following recommendations on the devolution of the SOTR to LGs: (a) the Commission recommended following the UFC's approach, namely that devolved funds are based on the estimate made for the year of devolution t; (b) it was recommended that appropriate changes may be effected in projected gross and the net SOTR, based on actual tax realization, and any excess or shortfall may be adjusted in devolution to the LGs in the subsequent years; (c) it was recommended that the award be given specifying the amount of money to be devolved to each LG for each year of the award period based on the t method; (d) rejecting the practice of giving a share of annual plan size of Kerala as development fund, the Commission recommended to give a share of net proceeds of SOTR as calculated on t basis; (e) the Commission had decided to distribute the maintenance fund to each LG on the basis of the actual road and non-road assets based on the Commission's assessments.

Vertical Devolution

The 5th SFC recommended that 20 per cent of the net proceeds of annual SOTR should be devolved to LGs as total devolution on (t) basis in the year 2016–2017. For the subsequent years, an annual increase of 1 per cent is recommended as shown in Table 8.1.

And the Commission recommended an award of ₹8,599.48 crore for the year 2016–2017. The recommendation for the subsequent years of the period are ₹10,105.94 crore for 2017–2018, ₹11,850.44 crore for 2018–2019, ₹13,868.59 crore for 2019–2020 and ₹16,201.19 crore for 2020–2021. This devolution excludes the grant given by the 14th UFC for civic services to LGs. The component-wise recommendations are shown in Table 8.2.

Table 8.1 *Total Devolution: Net SOTR on (t) Basis (%)*

Year	Net SOTR on (t) Basis (Share) (%)	General Purpose Fund (%)	Maintenance Fund (%)	Development Fund (%)
2016–2017	20	3.5	5.5	11.0
2017–2018	21	3.5	6.0	11.5
2018–2019	22	3.5	6.0	12.5
2019–2020	23	3.5	6.0	13.5
2020–2021	24	3.5	6.0	14.5

Source: State Finance Commission (2015).

Table 8.2 *Funds to be Devolved during 5th SFC Period (₹ in Crore)*

	2016–2017	2017–2018	2018–2019	2019–2020	2020–2021
GPF	1,504.91	1,684.33	1,885.30	2,110.44	2,362.68
Maintenance fund	2,364.86	2,887.41	3,231.94	3,617.89	4,050.30
Development fund	4,729.71	5,534.20	6,733.20	8,140.26	9,788.21
Total	8,599.48	10,105.94	11,850.44	13,868.59	16,201.19
SOTR	44,382.32	49,709.34	55,681.39	62,377.26	69,885.47
Net SOTR	42,997.28	48,123.47	53,865.57	60,298.15	67,504.89

Source: State Finance Commission (2015).

The Commission recommended devolution of funds for three purposes, namely general purpose, maintenance of assets and development.

General Purpose Fund

The 5th SFC recommended 3.5 per cent of the net SOTR on *t* basis per year as GPF (Table 8.1). The amount of funds recommended for GPF ranged between ₹1,504.91 crore and ₹2,362.68 crore between 2016–2017 and 2020–2021 (Table 8.2). GPF is primarily meant for meeting expenditure for the execution of the mandatory functions of

GPs, municipalities and MCs as stipulated in the KPRA, 1994, and the KMA, 1994, and other basic functions. Most of the mandatory functions are the traditional civic functions. However, it was recommended that the fund shall be used for the following purposes also: (a) to cover the deficit in own funds (tax and non-tax sources) for meeting administrative, establishment, operating and other items of expenditure of LGs; (b) to meet the items of recurring expenditure of the TIs which were met from the non-road maintenance fund up to the 4th SFC period such as electricity charges, water charges, fuel charges, purchase of furniture in government schools/hospitals, purchase of consumables in school labs, renewal of AMC of computers and purchase of medicines including veterinary medicines in emergency situations.

Maintenance Fund

The 5th SFC recommended 5.5 per cent of net SOTR as maintenance fund for the year 2016–2017 and 6 per cent per year for the subsequent four years (Table 8.1). The amount of maintenance fund recommended ranged between ₹2,364.86 crore and ₹4,050.30 crore between 2016–2017 and 2020–2021 (Table 8.2). Maintenance fund is meant for meeting the maintenance expenditure of the assets of TIs and LG's own institutions. Maintenance comprises the repairs and replacements of spare items plus other requirements needed to retain an asset in working condition. The Commission advocated the use of the fund for maintenance purposes only. Two categories of maintenance funds were recommended, namely (a) for road and (b) for non-road assets. Maintenance fund (road) would cover repair and maintenance of all types of roads of the LGs including roads constructed under Member of Parliament Local Area Development Scheme (MPLADS), MLA Fund, PMGSY, flood relief, etc., maintenance of culverts, bridges, etc., resurfacing/re-taring of existing roads, construction of drainage system, filling up of potholes and strengthening of embankments. Its use for creation/construction of new roads and also for upgradation of existing roads was not to be permitted. Maintenance fund (non-road) would cover repair and maintenance of all non-road assets including assets of TIs, hospital buildings, furniture, machineries and equipment, toilets, computers and allied equipment including AMC, and all other non-road assets including own assets.

Development Fund

The 5th SFC recommended 11 per cent of net SOTR as development fund for 2016–2017 (Table 8.1) and for the subsequent years, it ranged between 11.5 per cent to 14.5 per cent. The amount of funds recommended as development fund ranged between ₹4,729.71 crore and 9,788.21 crore between 2016–2017 and 2020–2021 (Table 8.2). Development fund is meant to finance the decentralized plans of the LGs for the local-level development. The individual LGs will have freedom to prepare and execute annual plans consisting of a number of individual projects and schemes for the local-level development, subject to the overall plan guideline of the state government.

Other Major Recommendations

The 14th UFC recommended grants to LGs for improving the delivery of basic services. The practice followed in Kerala is to transfer this as part of development fund. The 5th SFC disagreed with the practice. The Commission recommended that the grants given by the 14th UFC for civic services should be treated as a separate grant and it should be transferred in addition to the devolution of the Commission.

The Commission recommended that a GF shall be distributed to the financially weak GPs and ₹50 crore from the share of GPF available to the GPs is to be set apart for the purpose. Gap is calculated as follows: own fund plus GPF minus total of establishment, administrative, operations and other recurring expenses.

HORIZONTAL DEVOLUTION

General Purpose Fund

The Commission recommended that horizontal devolution of GPF should be effected as per the following criteria. For distributing share of various categories of LGs (GPs, BPs, DPs, municipalities and MCs) as well as individual LGs belonging to each category, the sharing criteria mentioned is as follows.

Share of DP and BP

1. First, the share of GPF of DPs and BPs is earmarked.
2. The total amount of DPs and BPs are to be calculated in the following manner.
   a. Amount given in the year 2015–2016 + annual incremental increase of 12 per cent for the 5th SFC period.
4. For inter se distribution of GPF to the DPs, weightage shall be given to population (50%), area (10%), number of government high schools (10%), higher secondary schools (10%) and number of district-level government hospitals coming under the DPs (20%).
5. For inter se distribution of GPF to BPs, weightage shall be given to population (70%), area (10%) and number of government hospitals coming under the BPs (20%).

Share of GPs, Municipalities and MCs

After deducting the total share of DPs and BPs, the balance will be distributed among GPs, municipalities and MCs on the basis of 2011 population detailed as follows: GPs (77.24%), municipalities (13.43%) and MCs (9.33%). The 5th SFC also decided to give SGs, one-time grants and revenue collection incentive bonus, to be deducted from the share of respective category of LGs.

Share of GPs

Share to be distributed to GPs = Total share of GPF – (a GF of ₹50 crore per annum + SG @ ₹15 lakh per annum given to six GPs + revenue collection incentive bonus of ₹5 crore per annum).

This share of GPs shall be distributed among GPs based on the following weightage (population 80%, area 10% and inverse of income 10%)

Share of Municipalities

Share to be distributed to municipalities = Total share of municipalities – (SG of ₹25 lakh per annum to Guruvayoor Municipality + one-time grant of ₹10 lakh per municipality to 28 new municipalities + revenue collection incentive bonus of ₹1 crore per annum).

The share of municipalities shall be distributed among municipalities based on the following weightage (population 80%, area 10% and inverse of income 10%).

Share of MCs

Share to be distributed to MCs = Total share of MCs – (one-time grant of ₹25 lakh to newly created Kannur Corporation for 2016–2017 + revenue collection incentives bonus of ₹50 lakh per annum).

The share of MCs shall be distributed among MCs based on the following weightage (population 80%, area 10% and inverse of income 10%).

Maintenance Fund

The 5th SFC recommended the horizontal devolution of maintenance fund as follows. For distributing share of various categories of LGs as well as individual LGs belonging to each category, the following sharing criteria (1) to (3) shall be followed.

1. The total maintenance fund of the LGs shall be divided into maintenance for road assets and non-road assets in the proportion of 78.1: 21.9.
2. The LG-wise sharing of the maintenance fund for each item of road and non-road will be on the basis of the following share. The share is worked out on the basis of the asset position of various categories of LGs as on 30 September 2015.

   The road and non-road assets were verified and corrected by the Commission and found that the total black topped (BT) road

Table 8.3 *Assets of LGs*

Category of LGs	Plinth Area of Building (in sq. m)	BT Road Length (in km)
DP	2,143,088.31	3,132.39
Municipality	1,314,693.90	10,751.51
BP	762,903.36	0.00
GP	3,874,188.88	47,184.71
MC	968,234.39	3,916.27
	9,063,108.84	**64,984.87**

Source: State Finance Commission (2015).

length under the custody of LGs was 64,984.87 km and total plinth area of buildings owned by LGs was 9,063,108.84 sq. m (Table 8.3).

3. The inter se share among the LGs shall be based on their respective share in road and non-road assets. LG-wise distribution of assets (road and non-road) is given in the report of the Commission (Appendix B, part II of the report).

Development Fund

The 5th SFC recommended the horizontal devolution and distribution of development fund into SCP fund, TSP fund and general sector fund as per sharing criteria prescribed as follows.

1. SCP fund based on the share of SC population to total population of 2011 Census.
2. TSP fund based on the share of ST population to total population of 2011 Census.
3. General sector fund which is the difference between total development fund and SCP and TSP fund.

Thus, total development fund = SCP fund + TSP fund + General sector fund

SCP Portion of Development Fund

The Commission recommended the horizontal devolution and distribution of SCP portion of development fund as per the sharing criteria prescribed as follows.

1. Total fund will be divided between rural and urban in the ratio of SC population of 2011 Census.
2. The SCP fund available for rural LGs will be divided among GP, BP and DP on the ratio of 60:20:20.
3. The inter se share among rural LGs shall be based on SC population.
4. The SCP fund available to urban LGs will be divided among municipalities and MCs on the basis of SC population.

TSP Portion of Development Fund

The Commission recommended the horizontal devolution and distribution of TSP portion of development fund as per the sharing criteria prescribed as follows.

1. Total fund will be divided between rural and urban in the ratio of ST population of 2011 Census.
2. The TSP fund available for rural LGs will be divided among GP, BP and DP on the ratio of 60:20:20.
3. The inter se share among rural LGs shall be based on ST population.
4. The TSP fund available to urban LGs will be divided among municipalities and MCs in the ratio of share of ST population.

General Sector Portion of Development Fund

The Commission recommended the horizontal devolution and distribution of general sector portion of development fund based on the criteria of distribution mentioned in Table 8.4.

Table 8.4 *Formula for Distribution of General Sector Portion of Development Fund*

Criteria	(Weightage in % by Type of LG)				
	GP	BP	DP	Municipality	MC
Population	60	60	60	60	60
Percentage of BPL households	20	20	20	20	20
Area	20	20	20	20	20
Total	100	100	100	100	100

Source: State Finance Commission (2015).

In Figures 8.1–8.4, the criteria used for overall horizontal devolution of GPF, maintenance fund and development fund and its inter se share is shown.

LG-WISE AND FUND-WISE DEVOLUTION OF FUNDS

The total amount recommended for different categories of LG from the share of SOTR (development, general purpose and maintenance fund) and UFC grant is given in Table 8.5.

All the categories of LGs are entitled to get development, general purpose and maintenance fund. In the case of UFC grants, only three categories of LGs—GPs, municipalities and MCs—are eligible for the

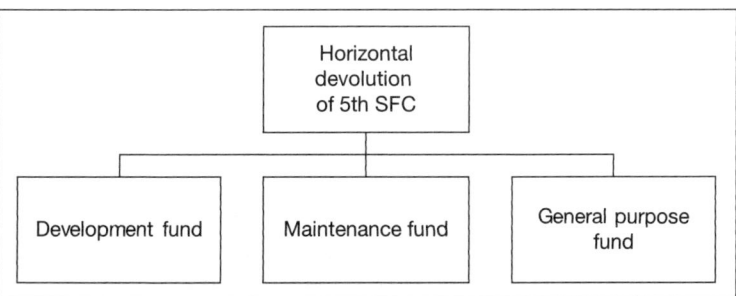

Figure 8.1 *Horizontal Devolution of 5th SFC*

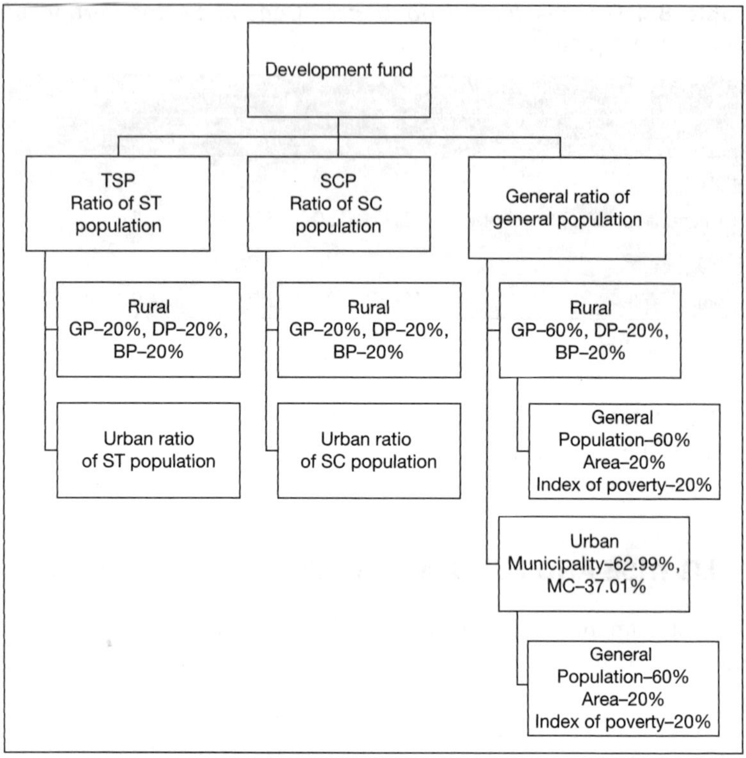

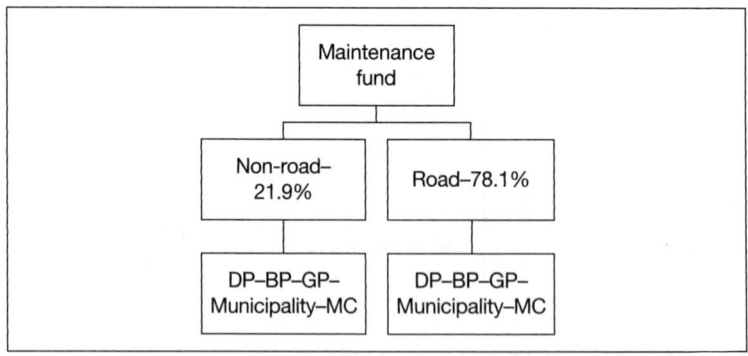

Figure 8.2 *Development Fund*

Figure 8.3 *Maintenance Fund*

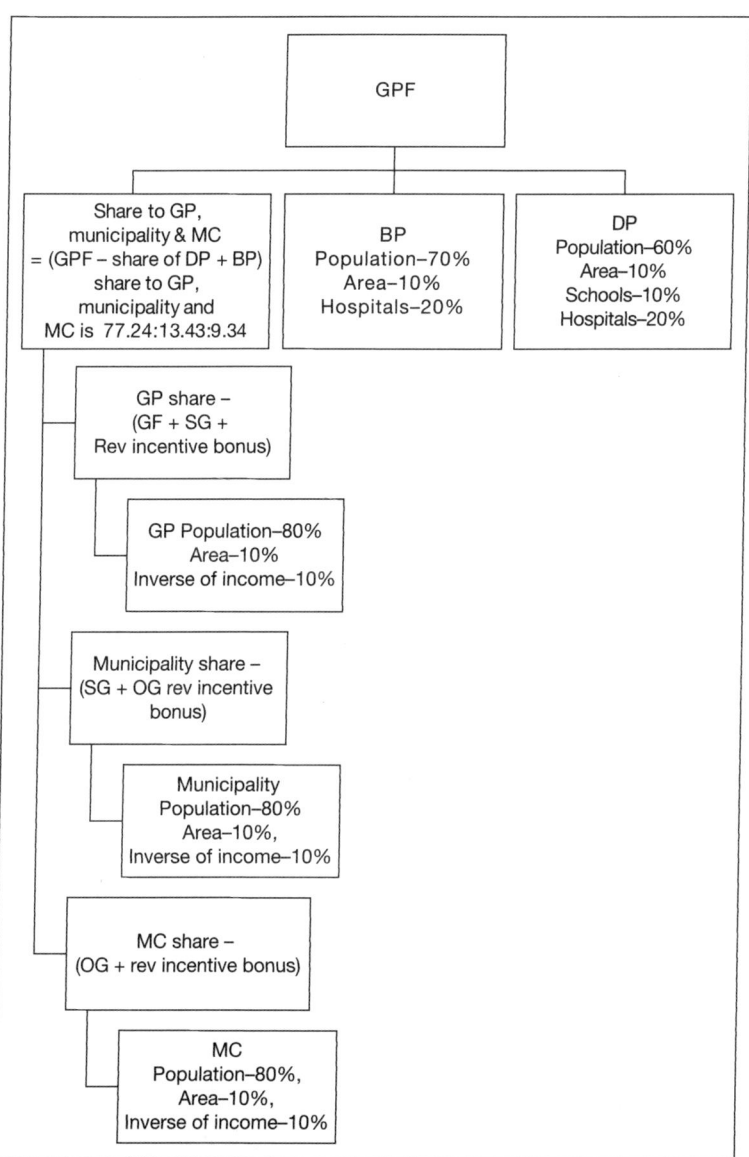

Figure 8.4 *General Purpose Fund*

Table 8.5 Total Transfer of Funds during the 5th SFC Period: LG Category-Wise (₹ in Crore)

Name	2016–2017	2017–2018	2018–2019	2019–2020	2020–2021
GP	**5,562.56**	**6,523.62**	**7,590.48**	**8,976.80**	**9,164.23**
Development fund	2,304.83	2,696.87	3,281.15	3,966.82	4,769.89
GPF	1,094.84	1,225.31	1,371.46	1,535.19	1,718.63
Maintenance fund	1,562.27	1,907.49	2,135.09	2,390.06	2,675.71
UFC grant	600.62	693.96	802.78	1,084.73	
Municipality	**1,446.45**	**1,697.50**	**1,977.40**	**2,382.75**	**2,108.01**
Development fund	559.00	654.08	795.79	962.08	1,156.85
GPF	190.57	213.29	238.73	267.23	299.16
Maintenance fund	380.69	464.81	520.27	582.40	652.00
UFC grant	316.19	365.33	422.62	571.05	
DP	**1,015.77**	**1,197.52**	**1,427.93**	**1,696.43**	**2,008.86**
Development fund	768.28	898.96	1,093.72	1,322.27	1,589.96
GPF	35.91	40.22	45.04	50.45	56.50
Maintenance fund	211.59	258.35	289.17	323.71	362.39

MC	799.25	934.42	1,090.81	1,315.95	1,175.00
Development fund	329.33	385.34	468.83	566.80	681.55
GPF	132.52	148.31	166.00	185.82	208.02
Maintenance fund	166.66	203.49	227.77	254.96	285.44
UFC grant	170.75	197.28	228.22	308.37	
BP	**862.99**	**1,009.44**	**1,217.42**	**1,460.79**	**1,745.07**
Development fund	768.28	898.96	1,093.72	1,322.27	1,589.96
GPF	51.07	57.20	64.06	71.75	80.36
Maintenance fund	43.64	53.28	59.64	66.76	74.74
Grand total	**9,687.02**	**11,362.50**	**13,304.04**	**15,832.72**	**16,201.17**

Source: State Finance Commission (2015).

grant. The total funds recommended by the 5th SFC increased from ₹9,687.02 crore in 2016–2017 to ₹16,201.17 crore in 2020–2021. An LG-wise growth and composition of transfer of funds recommended by the 5th SFC is given in Table 8.6.

From Table 8.6, we may draw the following inferences: (a) the annual growth of funds was more than 14 per cent in all categories of LGs between 2016–2017 and 2019–2020; (b) the growth rate of 2.27 per cent in 2020–2021 is attributed to non-availability of data of the UFC grant, to be recommended by the 15th UFC; (c) of the total transferred funds, the share of funds allocated to GPs is about 57 per cent, municipalities 15 per cent and MCs 8 per cent. These LGs are executing more functions such as mandatory, civic, maintenance of assets and development compared to other categories of LGs; (d) on the other hand, the LGs which are executing development and maintenance functions such as BPs and DPs get a lower share of the total funds.

STATUS OF IMPLEMENTATION

The 5th SFC submitted the first part of its report containing the recommendations on devolution in December 2015 and second part on other subjects in March 2016 to the Governor of Kerala. The award period of the Commission was five years from 2016–2017 to 2020–2021. But the Action Taken Report on the recommendations of the Commission was placed in Kerala Legislative Assembly on 7 February 2018. Hence, the state government delayed the presentation of the Action Taken Report to the Kerala legislature by two years. The state government failed to devolve funds to the 1,200 LGs in Kerala based on 5th SFC recommendations in two budgets for the years 2016–2017 and 2017–2018. The government also allotted a lower amount than the amount recommended by the 5th SFC for three consecutive years. The amount allotted to LGs was 10 per cent less in 2016–2017, 14 per cent less in 2017–2018 and 19 per cent less in 2018–2019. And the 1,200 LGs in Kerala were denied their legitimate right to receive their due share of state taxes recommended by the 5th SFC for three years.

Table 8.6 LG Category-Wise Transfer of Funds: Growth and Composition

Sl No.	Category of LGs	2016–2017	2017–2018	2018–2019	2019–2020	2020–2021
			Growth (%)			
1	GP	–	14.73	14.06	18.26	2.05
2	Municipality	–	14.79	14.15	20.50	–13.03
3	DP	–	15.18	16.14	15.83	15.55
4	MC	–	14.47	16.74	17.11	–12.00
5	BP	–	14.51	17.08	16.66	16.29
	Total	–	14.75	14.59	15.97	2.27
			Composition (%)			
1	GP	57.42	57.41	57.05	56.70	56.57
2	Municipality	14.93	14.94	14.86	15.05	13.01
3	DP	10.49	10.54	10.73	10.71	12.40
4	MC	8.25	8.23	8.20	8.31	7.25
5	BP	8.91	8.88	9.16	9.23	10.77
	Total	100	100	100	100	100

Source: Based on Table 8.5.

Rejection of Devolution Recommendation

It is disturbing to note that all the core devolution recommendations of the Commission were rejected by the state government. They include devolution of funds based on the year of devolution t followed by UFC, recommendations of devolved funds to each LG for the award period, distribution of maintenance fund based on actual assets of the LG, unhealthy diversion of maintenance fund for non-maintenance purpose, distribution of a share of SOTR as development fund, treating 14th UFC grants as separate grant, etc. Table 8.7 gives the list of core devolution recommendations of the 5th SFC rejected by the state government.

Table 8.7 *Major Devolution Recommendations Rejected by State Government*

1	Devolution of funds based on the estimate made for the year of devolution t following UFC approach.
2	Any excess or shortfall may be adjusted in devolution to LGs in subsequent years based on tax realization.
3	Award recommending the amount of money to be devolved to each LG for each year of the award period based on the t method.
4	3.5% of the net proceeds of the annual SOTR be devolved as GPF on t basis for five years.
5	Distribute the maintenance fund to each LG on the basis of the actual road and non-road assets based on commission's assessment.
6	5.5–6% of the net SOTR on t basis as maintenance fund.
7	Maintenance fund should be used only for the purpose of maintenance of road and non-road assets.
8	A share of the net proceeds of the SOTR—as calculated on t basis—as the development fund. The rate of devolution recommended ranged between 11% and 14.5%.
9	The grants given by the 14th UFC for civic services to LGs be treated as a separate grant and transferred in addition to the devolution of the Commission.
10	Transfer the devolved funds to public accounts of LGs in 12 instalments in a year.

Instead of opting for a progressive criterion suggested by the 5th SFC, the state government decided to continue with the existing practice of devolving SOTR based on the tax receipts of two years back. The government is not prepared to change the norms of distribution of maintenance fund to LGs based on reliable data of assets. This results in distorted distribution of maintenance funds in that LGs with small amount assets get larger share and LGs with large amount assets get small share.

Recommendations Accepted and Rejected

The 5th SFC had given 133 recommendations based on the ToR of the Commission. Based on the action taken on each of the recommendation, we have classified them as accepted, rejected and accepted with modifications. The recommendations comes under the items such as devolution of SOTR, maintenance of assets, UFC grants, mobilization of own resources, finances of rural and urban LGs, implementation of the previous SFC recommendations, fiscal issues, restructuring plan and changes in law, rules and procedures. Table 8.8 gives the number of recommendations accepted, accepted with modification and rejected.

Of the total recommendations, 59 per cent were accepted by the state government. In the case of recommendations on devolution, the percentage of acceptance is very small (14%). Of the total recommendations on change in law, rules and procedures, 50 per cent were accepted. The other items of recommendations, majority of which accepted, were fiscal issues, UFC grants, finances of rural LGs and mobilization of own resources. An interesting aspect is the acceptance of 94 per cent of the recommendations of the first four SFCs which were accepted by the successive state governments but not operationalized so far. From the preceding text, we can conclude that most of the recommendations on devolution, maintenance of assets and finances of urban LGs were rejected. However, the government accepted 79 per cent of the recommendations on mobilization of own resources of LGs.

Table 8.8 5th SFC: Number of Recommendations Accepted and Rejected

Sl No.	Item	Total Number of Recommendations	Number of Accepted	Number of Accepted with Modification	Number of Rejected	Percentage of Accepted to Total
1	Devolution of SOTR	21	3	4	14	14.29
2	Maintenance of assets	5	1	1	3	20.00
3	UFC grants	5	3	–	2	60.00
4	Mobilization of own resources of LGs	29	23	1	5	79.31
5	Finances of rural LGs	3	2	1	–	66.67
6	Finances of municipalities and MCs	3	–	1	2	–
7	Implementation of previous SFC recommendations	32	30	–	2	93.75
8	Fiscal issues	12	7	2	3	58.34
9	Restructuring plan formulation and execution	13	4	3	6	30.77
10	Change in law, rules and procedures	10	5	–	5	50.00
	Total	133	78	13	42	58.65

Source: Government of Kerala (2018).

CONCLUSIONS

The 5th SFC's approach to devolution is much different from the approaches followed by the earlier SFCs. In place of devolution based on $(t-2)$ or $(t-3)$ method, the Commission used t method for devolving state taxes based on the year of devolution. Instead of giving maintenance fund based on unreliable data, the Commission decided to distribute the maintenance fund to each LG on the basis of the actual road and non-road assets. Regarding the practice of giving a share of annual plan size of Kerala as development fund, the Commission recommended to give a share of net proceeds of SOTR as development fund. The 5th SFC wanted to treat the grants of 14th UFC given to LGs as a separate grant and it should be transferred to LGs in addition to SFC's devolution. The Commission also recommended that the award is to be given specifying the amount of money to be devolved to each LG for each year of the award period.

Clear norms are prescribed for the horizontal devolution of GPF, maintenance fund and development fund for various categories of LGs as well as for individual LG. Based on the earlier devolution principles and criteria, the Commission had worked out item-wise and year-wise amount of devolution to the 1,200 LGs of Kerala for a period of five years.

However, the state government delayed the placement of Action Taken Report in the Kerala State Legislature assembly by more than two years and delayed its implementation. The government was not prepared to devolve funds to the 1,200 LGs based on the 5th SFC for three years (2016–2017 to 2018–2019). The government allotted funds to LGs arbitrarily, rejecting the 5th SFC recommendations. It is disturbing to note that except a few (14%), all the recommendations on devolution were rejected. A deliberate attempt was made by the finance department to delay its implementation and reject its core devolution recommendations and sabotage the fiscal decentralization process in Kerala.

The delayed implementation of the 5th SFC and rejection of most of the devolution recommendations raised many serious issues. The recommendations of the 5th SFC, a constitutional body, was not implemented for two years. The 1,200 LGs in Kerala were denied their legitimate right to receive their due share of state taxes recommended by the 5th SFC for three years. The government allotted a lower amount than the amount recommended by the 5th SFC for three consecutive years. Most of the core devolution recommendations of the 5th SFC which are formulated based on clear norms for general purpose, maintenance of assets and development were rejected. The fiscal decentralization system in Kerala is subverted. There is arbitrary allocation of resources, reversal of fiscal decentralization and move towards fiscal centralization. We can consider this as a black chapter in the history of Kerala's decentralization.

Decentralized Planning

Plan Performance of Gram Panchayats

In this chapter, we examine the plan performance, namely plan formulation, execution and achievement of financial targets of GPs. The chapter is divided into three sections, namely (a) introduction, (b) plan formulation and execution guidelines and (c) plan performance of GPs.

INTRODUCTION

In India, the basic structure of administrative system at the centre and states has been designed for centralized governance. The transformation of this system to decentralization is a challenging and very difficult task. Kerala's decentralization is basically developmental. Decentralized planning has been used as an instrument for accelerating the process of decentralization. Though Kerala has succeeded in evolving a methodology of the local-level planning, it has not succeeded in implementing annual plans efficiently and in a time-bound manner. The 73rd and 74th Amendments of the Constitution of India have enhanced the role of rural and urban LGs and assigned responsibility for preparation of plans for economic development and social justice. The KPRA, 1994, and the KMA, 1994, also assigned the role of formulation and implementation of development plans for economic development and social justice to panchayats and municipalities.

The successive SFCs have given high priority for development and recommended major share of devolved funds for development purposes. The 5th SFC recommended more than half of the devolved funds for financing the development plans of the LGs. Though the LGs have been preparing and executing development plans for the last two decades, majority of them have not been able to perform satisfactorily due to a number of factors. Poor plan performance on all fronts, namely plan formulation, execution, monitoring, achievement of physical and financial targets, etc., may be identified as the most important problem faced by the LGs during the last two decades.

In this context, an attempt is made to examine the causes for the poor plan performance of GPs.

In order to examine plan performance, we have used the data from the 5th SFC. For examining the plan performance, we have used indicators such as date of constitution of working groups, date of meeting of the working groups, date of meeting of gram sabha/ward sabha, date of development seminar, date of approval of annual plan by the council of LG, date of approval of DPC, category of projects implemented (contractor and beneficiary committee), percentage of projects completed in a year, percentage of fund utilization (plan and maintenance), and quarter-wise and month-wise spending of the plan. As separate data are not available about the annual outlay of development plan and expenditure, we have taken the fund availability and expenditure of development plan and maintenance.

Decentralized Planning: Objectives and Issues

The basic objectives of decentralized planning pursued during the last four Five-Year Plans are the following: (a) promotion of local economic development by enhancing production and productivity of agriculture and allied sectors, traditional and small-scale industries with focus on employment and poverty reduction; (b) reduction in gender disparities; (c) integrated area development; (d) improving governance, especially in terms of transparency, people's participation and responsiveness; (e) bringing about an organic relationship between transferred departments and LGs, and bring in role clarity; (f) achieving the sustainable local-level development through preservation of ecology, environment and natural resources; (g) infrastructure development (provision of housing, drinking water, electricity, better transport facilities, health services, clean environment for all and sanitation including solid waste management) to achieve better quality of life for all; (h) improving the delivery of public services (hospitals, schools, anganwadis, etc.) and (i) improving the welfare of marginalized and vulnerable sections of people (women, children, the elderly people, SC/ST categories, traditional fishermen and those employed in traditional industries).

The 4th SFC had examined the decentralized planning of LGs and identified certain serious issues in plan formulation and implementation. They are: (a) tendency to divide the devolved funds ward-wise leading to relatively small projects being taken up; (b) plans appear to emerge from negotiated priorities than from participatory situation analysis based on data and experience; (c) working groups and technical advisory groups, the instruments of preparation of plans, are becoming perfunctory; (d) planning and implementation of SCP and TSP is far below the desired levels; (e) although 10 per cent of the general sector expenditure has to be spent as Women Component Plan (WCP), the realization of desirable outcome is poor. The planning and implementation of WCP is below expectations; (f) significant improvement in the horizontal and vertical integration of plans is needed; (g) poor record of service delivery in public institutions; (h) focus continues to lie on LG level plan and annual plan; (i) no significant achievement in the production sector and local economic development sector; (j) absence of effective system of quality assurance for concurrent monitoring; (k) weak role of intermediate panchayats and (l) DPCs still function as committees with emphasis on project clearance of LGs.

PLAN FORMULATION AND EXECUTION GUIDELINES

Project Identification and Finalization Phase

A development plan comprises a list of economically, financially and technologically feasible projects and schemes. Preparation of financially feasible and implementable type of project is a precondition of a good development plan. The plan should also be supported by adequate resources. Review of the current situation of the local economy and its problems, identification of development requirements, fixing the priorities of development and preparing feasible projects are the initial stages involved in the planning process.

The procedure prescribed for the various stages of plan formulation and execution is discussed further. Though the procedure was prescribed by the state government in the initial stages of implementing decentralized plans in the second half of the 1990s, the practice continued without much change till 2013. Some marginal changes in the procedure were effected in November 2013. The procedure which is being followed at present in the pre-project formulation stage is given in Table 9.1. The time frame given for various steps in plan formulation is also given in Table 9.1. The first step in plan formulation is appointment of plan coordinators and working groups. According to the guidelines issued by the state government, a GP will have to constitute 13 working groups on finance, development, social welfare, education, health, etc. The second step is to prepare a status report of the plan comprising project proposals. The third step is consultation with banks and other stakeholders about the proposed plan. The fourth step is the discussion of development issues, problems and project proposals at the gram/ward sabhas. Guidelines are issued about the procedure to be followed in the conduct of gram sabhas (Table 9.2). The fifth step is finalization of status report, project proposals and preparation of a draft development plan.

The second phase in the plan formulation process is preparation of a development document, conducting development seminar, approval of development document, plan allocation, preparation of plan projects and approval of plan projects. Table 9.3 gives the various steps in the plan formulation in the second phase. Thus, the earlier elaborate, time-consuming and irrelevant plan procedure is prescribed to identify the projects. The actual preparation of projects starts only after observing these numerous procedures mentioned earlier.

According to the guidelines issued, the total time given for the preparation of all projects of an annual plan in a financial year is 35 days during the first year of the Five-Year Plan. During the subsequent years, the number of days given for preparation of all projects of an annual plan is 15 days (25 December to 10 January). It is humanly

Table 9.1 *Plan Formulation Process (First Phase)*

Sl No.	Steps	Committee/Group Responsible	Target Dates for Plan Preparation
1	Appointment of plan coordinator	Committee/Council of LGs	Before 20 November (if needed)
2	Constituting working groups	Implementing officer (recommending); Standing committees (recommending); Administrative Committee (approving)	Before 25 November
3	Preparation of district-wise priority list		25 November
4	Preparation of status report including project plan	Standing committee; working groups	If necessary
5	Discussion with bank	Standing committees; working groups; administrative committees	If necessary
6	Discussion with stakeholders	Working groups; standing committees	If necessary
7	Rapid assessment	Working groups; standing committees	Before 25 November
8	Gram sabhas/ward sabhas	Working group members; facilitators; administrative committee; ward member/councillor	Before 15 December
9	Finalization of status report and project suggestions preparation	Working groups; standing committees	Before 15 December (status report is not applicable for coming years)

Source: Local Self Government Department (2013).

Table 9.2 *Programme Schedule of Gram/Ward Sabha*

1	Welcome (5 minute)	Gram sabha convener
2	Development views of panchayat (10 minutes)	President/vice-president
3	Rights and duties of grama sabha (10 minutes)	Resource person
4	Plan implementation report of current year and previous year (10 minutes)	Secretary/plan coordinator
5	Presentation of draft project suggestions of next year (10 minutes)	Development standing committee chair person/welfare standing committee chairperson
6	General discussion and question answers (previous plan activities, activities of organizations and employees, decisions of gram sabha, general administration, etc.; 45 minutes)	Questions may be collected in the meeting or earlier in writing. Participants may also be permitted to raise questions.
7	Group discussion (draft project proposals; 90 minutes)	Discussions may be done in groups based on the number of working groups. Service of a facilitator may be made available by panchayat in each group.
8	Reporting of group discussion (plenary session; 30 minutes)	Presentation of the proposals of the group
9	General discussion on draft plan (15 minutes)	
10	Summing of discussions	President/vice-president/standing committee chairperson
11	Approval of written minutes, putting signature	Apart from people's representatives and officials, anybody who attended gram sabha can sign
12	Conclusion, vote of thanks	Gram sabha coordinator/secretary

- Urban local bodies should also conduct ward sabha meetings as per this schedule.
- BPs–DPs may conduct gram sabha meetings as per this schedule as mentioned in Panchayat Rule 15. But item 3 of this schedule may be excluded

Source: Local Self Government Department (2013).

Table 9.3 Plan Formulation Process (Second Phase)

Sl No.	Steps	Committee/Group Responsible	Target Dates for Plan Preparation
1	Development document (in the Five-Year Plan period and annual plan document)	Working group; development standing committees	Development document (NA for coming years)
2	Preparation of integrated programmes	Working groups; standing committees	If necessary
3	Development seminar	Administrative committee; development standing committee	Before 15 December
4	Approval of development document	Administrative committee	NA
5	Decision on plan provision and allocation of plan total	Administrative committee; finance standing committee	Before 30 December
6	Preparation of project	Working groups	Before 10 January
7	Approval of projects by standing committees	Standing committees	Before 15 January
8	Approval of plan projects	Administrative committees	Before 20 January
9	Approval of plan projects	DPC	–

Source: Local Self Government Department (2013).

impossible to prepare all projects of an annual plan of a GP or municipality within this period with the few engineering and other staff available with them and the staff belonging to TIs.

Approvals and Technical Sanctions

The second major stage in the preparation of a development plan is scrutiny, approval and giving technical sanctions to projects that are engineering in nature. Initial preparation will have to be done by the assistant engineer in a GP or municipality. The scrutiny or approval of the projects will have to be done by an engineer at a higher level in BP or DP. Similarly, in MCs having a superintending engineer, all the projects will have to be sent to chief engineer, LSGD.

Table 9.4 gives the hierarchy of engineers who have the power to scrutinize and approve construction-related projects. The approved projects will have to be sent to the DPC for approval. After getting the approval of the DPC, the projects will have to be sent to engineers

Table 9.4 *Scrutiny and Approval of Construction-Related Projects*

Sl No.	Projects of Rural and Urban LG	Engineer Who Is Authorized to Approve
1	Projects of GPs	Assistant executive engineer of BP
2	Projects of BPs	Executive engineer of DP
3	Projects of DPs	Superintending engineer (decided by chief engineer)
4	The project of municipalities having assistant engineer as municipal engineer	Assistant executive engineer of BPs
5	The projects of municipalities having assistant executive engineer as municipal engineer	Executive engineers
6	The projects of municipalities having executive engineer as municipal engineer	Superintending engineer (decided by chief engineer)
7	Projects of MCs	Chief engineer of LSGD

Source: Local Self Government Department (2013).

for technical sanction. In the case of majority of the LGs, the detailed project estimates will be prepared only at this stage. Table 9.5 gives the engineers authorization for giving technical sanction.

Thus, four levels of clearances are required for qualifying a project for actual implementation, namely (a) the initial preparation of a project by an assistant engineer of an LG, (b) scrutiny and approval by an engineer at a higher level, (c) approval of the projects by DPC and (d) issue of technical sanction by competent engineers. Thus, considerable time is required for this process of getting approvals or clearances from the various hierarchy of engineers.

Execution of Projects

The third major stage is execution of projects. Compared to the earlier stages, this is the most difficult stage. The first step in execution is tendering a project or identifying a beneficiary committee. Once the formalities of the tender process are completed, the LG can award the work to a contractor, or entrust it to a beneficiary committee. Supervising the execution of work, especially construction-related work, is a challenging task. The flooding of execution of work during the last quarter of the financial year creates serious problems in

Table 9.5 *Engineers Authorized for Giving Technical Sanction*

Sl No.	Projects	Engineer Who Is Authorized to Approve
1	The projects of GPs and municipalities which have the assistant engineer as municipal engineer	Assistant executive engineer of the BP (the executive engineer DP will decide the AEE)
2	The projects of BPs and municipalities which have the assistant executive engineer as municipal engineer	Executive engineer of DP
3	The projects of DPs and municipalities which have the executive engineer as municipal engineer	Superintending engineer (LSGD chief engineer will decide the SE)
4	The projects of MC	Chief engineer/LSGD

Source: Local Self Government Department (2013).

supervision. Lack of adequate staff, both engineers and overseers, is also a serious constraint. It is also the duty of the executing staff to ensure that good quality work has been done by the contractor/beneficiary committee. The last step in execution is the preparation and payment of bills to the contractors/beneficiary committees. Table 9.6 gives the various steps involved in the execution of the projects.

Annual Plan Expenditure of Rural LGs in Kerala

A review of annual plan outlay and expenditure of the rural LGs, namely GPs, BPs and DPs for 2014–2015 is given in Table 9.7.

Of the total plan outlay of ₹3,842 crore, the percentage of plan expenditure at the categories was 46. In the case of GPs, the percentage of expenditure was 46. The percentage of expenditure of the BPs and the DPs were 53 and 42, respectively. This indicates very poor

Table 9.6 *Project Execution*

Step	Committee/Officer Responsible
Project execution—First stage	Tendering/identifying beneficiary committee
Project execution—Second stage	Finalization of tender/award of work to contractor/beneficiary committee
Execution of work—Supervision	Designated officer/engineer
Completion of the work	Verification by designated officer
Payment of bills	Implementing officer/finance officer of LGs

Table 9.7 *Annual Plan Expenditure of Rural LGs 2014–2015*

LG	Outlay (₹ in Crore)	Expenditure (₹ in Crore)	% of Expenditure	Average Number of Projects Executed
GP	2,595.59	1,185.05	46	116
BP	622.99	332.58	53	49
DP	622.99	261.49	42	733
Total	3,841.57	1,779.12	46	–

plan expenditure of the all categories of rural LGs. There are several reasons for the low plan fund utilization. But a major reason for this is the formulation and execution of very large number of projects which are beyond the administrative capacity of an LG. The average number of projects executed by GPs was 116, BPs 49 and DPs 773. Due to this, LGs were not able to complete the execution of a good part of the projects of an annual plan during the financial year, which become spillover projects subsequently. And the LGs will have to struggle for the completion of the spillover projects as well as new projects during the subsequent financial year.

PLAN PERFORMANCE OF SAMPLE GPS

We have examined the performance of annual plans of 15 sample GPs belonging to five districts, namely Thiruvananthapuram, Kollam, Ernakulam, Thrissur and Kozhikode. The sampling procedure followed to select the GPs is as follows: we identified five districts on the basis of the regions, namely south, central and northern. From each district, we selected three GPs located in the coastal region, the midland and the highlands on a sample basis. Data were collected from them based on a detailed interview schedule. We have discussed the plan activities with the officials, engineers and office-bearers of the GPs responsible for plan formulation and execution and visited a few GPs to see the execution of plan projects. The profile of the sample GPs such as number of wards, area in sq. km, location, population and number of BPL households are given in Table 9.8. The number of wards in the GPs ranged between 14 and 23. The GPs located in the highland or hilly regions have large area compared to others. Of the 15 sample GPs, 7 are located in coastal area, 5 in midland and 3 in highland or hilly areas. The population in the sample GPs ranged from 17,396 to 49,348 persons. The number of BPL households which are eligible for food, education, medical subsidies and other concessions are also given in Table 9.8.

Plan Formulation Stage

The plan formulation may be classified into two stages, namely project identification and project preparation and finalization of annual

Table 9.8 Area and Population of Sample GPs

Sl No.	Name of GP	Number of Wards	Area in Sq. Km	Location (Coastal/ Midland/Highland)	Population (in Number)	BPL Households
				Thiruvananthapuram district		
1	Kottukal	19	12.19	Coastal	33,336	5,442
2	Anchuthengu	14	3.36	Coastal	17,396	3,226
3	Vithura	17	131.56	Highland	26,249	4,584
				Kollam district		
4	Kottamkara	21	10.63	Midland	39,635	3,849
5	Kadakkal	19	29.9	Midland	30,719	3,677
6	Alappad	16	7.38	Coastal	21,655	3,061
				Ernakulam district		
7	Edavanakkad	15	10.17	Coastal	21,787	2,779
8	Cheranalloor	17	10.59	Midland	30,594	2,306
9	Kuttampuzha	17	543.07	Highland	24,451	4,480

			Thrissur district		
10	Erumapetty	18	32.12	Midland	29,834	3,301
11	Nattika	14	9.608	Coastal	19,406	1,599
12	Puthur	23	77.00	Midland, highland	49,284	5,452
			Kozhikode district		
13	Narippatta	17	50.63	Coastal	26,529	2,568
14	Kadalundi	22	12.02	Coastal	45,516	2,997
15	Unnikulam	23	38.26	Midland	49,348	4,516

plan. In the first stage, a review of the development problems of the GPs and identification of the areas which need urgent short-term or long-term measures are undertaken. After having discussions with the stakeholders and the gram sabha (the voters in a ward of a GP), the working group identifies the areas which need projects. Actual project preparation and approval by the committee of GP is the second stage. As per the plan guidelines issued by the GoK, a number of procedures have to be followed in the first stage of plan formulation (Table 9.1). The data collected from the sample GPs on date of appointment of plan coordinator, the number of working groups constituted, date of working group meeting, date of stakeholders meeting (SHM) and number of participants in SHM are given in Table 9.9.

Of the 15 GPs studied, 11 appointed the plan coordinators during the preceding year of the plan year. In two GPs, it was done during April 2014 and August 2014. The number of working groups constituted ranged from 11 to 13. Our discussion with the GPs revealed that the working groups are not contributing much to the plan formulation or identification of projects except in the case of few GPs. From the stakeholder consultations, the GPs are not getting the desired results. Of the 15 GPs, 5 have not conducted the meetings. The participation in the meetings is very poor in the case of majority of the meetings.

According to the KPRA, 1994, and KMA, 1994, gram sabhas are given an important role in identifying the development issues and suggesting project proposal for the local-level development. The GPs reported that they used to convene a meeting of gram sabha exclusively for the discussion of the issues related to annual plan. Table 9.10 gives the months in which gram sabhas met, the average number of participants, date of development seminar and number of participants. The gram sabhas met during December 2013, January and February 2014, except in one GP. The average number of participants in the gram sabhas ranged between 104 and 204 in the GPs studied. But it is pointed out that majority of the participants were women. In a good number of GPs, the average number of women participants ranged between 70 and 80 per cent. Majority of participants were persons connected with the activities of GPs such as MGNREGA workers, Kudambashree members and beneficiaries of housing and other

Table 9.9 Constitution of Working Groups for Plan Formulation in 2014–2015 in GPs

Sl No.	Name of GP	Date of Appointment of Plan Coordinator	No. of Working Groups	Date of Working Group Conducted	Date of Stakeholders Meeting	No. of Participants in Stakeholder Meeting
			Thiruvananthapuram district			
1	Kottukal	8 Jan 2014	12	22 Feb 2014	13 May 2014	16
2	Anchuthengu	1 Aug 2014	13	1 Oct 2014	NA	NA
3	Vithura	30 Apr 2014	13	8 July 2014	NA	NA
			Kollam district			
4	Kottamkara	18 Dec 2013	13	28 Dec 2013	4 Jan 2014	11
5	Kadakkal	22 Nov 2013	11	9 Jan 2014	28 Feb 2014	16
6	Alappad	5 Nov 2013	13	17 Dec 2013	17 Dec 2014	10
			Ernakulam district			
7	Edavanakkad	12 Nov 2013	13	21 Jan 2014	19 Jan 2014	22
8	Cheranalloor	10 July 2013	11	22 Jan 2014	1 Mar 2014	26
9	Kuttampuzha	NA	13	NA	NA	NA

(Continued)

Table 9.9 (Continued)

Sl No.	Name of GP	Date of Appointment of Plan Coordinator	No. of Working Groups	Date of Working Group Conducted	Date of Stakeholders Meeting	No. of Participants in Stakeholder Meeting
			Thrissur district			
10	Erumapetty	6 Nov 2013	12	22 Dec 2013	1 Feb 2014	37
11	Nattika	28 Nov 2013	12	7 Dec 2013	30 Jan 2014	15
12	Puthur	7 Nov 2013	13	10 Dec 2013	12 Jan 2014	101
			Kozhikode district			
13	Narippatta	25 Oct 2013	13	24 Dec 2013	NA	NA
14	Kadalundi	NA	13	23 Dec 2013	NA	NA
15	Unnikulam	28 Oct 2013	12	29 Nov 2013 5 Feb 2014	10 Dec 2013	67

Table 9.10 *Gram Sabha and Development Seminar in GPs for 2014–2015*

Sl No.	Name of GP	Month in Which Grama Sabha Met	Average No. of Participants	Date of Development Seminar	No. of Participants in Development Seminar
			Thiruvananthapuram district		
1	Kottukal	Feb 2014	131	31 May 2014	175
2	Anchuthengu	Jan 2014	104	2 May 2014	75
3	Vithura	Aug 2014	204	8 July 2014	NA
			Kollam district		
4	Kottamkara	Jan 2014	134	20 May 2014	127
5	Kadakkal	Jan 2014	137	26 Feb 2014	NA
6	Alappad	Dec 2013	126	15 Jan 2014	200
			Ernakulam district		
7	Edavanakkad	Jan 2014	110	28 Jan 2014	110
8	Cheranalloor	Feb 2014	127	28 Feb2014	67
9	Kuttampuzha	NA	NA	1 Feb 2014	NA

(Continued)

Table 9.10 (Continued)

Sl No.	Name of GP	Month in Which Grama Sabha Met	Average No. of Participants	Date of Development Seminar	No. of Participants in Development Seminar
			Thrissur district		
10	Erumapetty	Dec 2013	135	23 Dec 2013	71
11	Nattika	Dec 2013	120	25 Jan 2014	160
12	Puthur	Dec 2013	177	30 Feb 2013	128
			Kozhikode district		
13	Narippatta	Jan 2014	129	27 Jan 2014	NA
14	Kadalundi	Jan 2014	146	12 Feb 2014	203
15	Unnikulam	Jan 2014	155	12 Feb 2014	228

schemes meant for the poor. Only a few persons who attended discussed the development problems, project needed, etc. Except a few, all the GPs told us that the gram sabhas are not contributing much to the projects and schemes to be included in the annual plan of the LG.

The second step in the plan formulation process is preparation of a development document, preparation of integrated programmes, conduct of development seminar, approval of development document, allocation of plan resources and preparation of projects. The GPs told us that they are not bothered to adhere to the procedure of preparing a development document, integrated programme, etc. But all of them conducted development seminars. Majority of them conducted the seminar during the month of January and February 2014 prior to the financial year 2014–2015. But four GPs conducted development seminar in May and July of 2014. This indicates that the four GPs were not able to complete the preliminary procedure in annual plan preparation even after the commencement of the financial year in April 2014.

The next step is the preparation of projects and getting approval from the administrative committees of GPs. In the plan formulation guidelines, adequate time is not given for actual preparation of projects to be included in the annual plan. Ten to fifteen days are given for project preparation in the month of January for the annual plan starting from 1 April. It is stipulated that the approvals of the plan projects should be completed by 20 January. It is not possible to prepare all the projects within a few days. Further, January to March is the peak period of execution of the projects of the financial year. The data supplied by the sample GPs reveal that only 7 sample GPs were able to give approval of annual plan before March 2014 (Table 9.11). On the other hand, 7 sample GPs approved the annual plan for 2014–2015, in May 2014 (2 GPs), June 2014 (4 GPs) and October 2014 (1 GP). This delay in the approval of the annual plan is a major reason for the delayed execution and non-completion of projects during the financial year.

As per plan formulation guidelines, the GPs have to obtain the approval of plan projects from the DPC. The data supplied by the sample GPs reveal that the DPCs gave approval of the projects meant for 2014–2015 during a period ranging between February 2014 and March 2015 (Table 9.11). Of the total 15 GPs, 7 obtained approval for

Table 9.11 Date of Approval of Annual Plan Projects of GPs by Committee and DPC for 2014–2015

Sl No.	Name of GP	Date of Approval of Annual Plan by Panchayat Committee	Date of Approval by DPC	Period of Starting Execution of Projects
Thiruvananthapuram district				
1	Kottukal	16 Jun 2014	7 Nov 2014	Since January
2	Anchuthengu	2 Jun 2014	25 Feb 2014 17 Mar 2015 31 Mar 2015 2 Jul 2014	Since June
3	Vithura	6 Oct 2014	26 Jun 2014 30 Dec 2014 31 Mar 2015	Since July
Kollam district				
4	Kottamkara	23 Jun 2014	2 Jul 2014	Since October
5	Kadakkal	3 Mar 2014	27 Jun 2014 16 Mar 2015	Since August
6	Alappad	6 May 2014	27 June 2014 29 Jan 2015	NA
Ernakulam district				
7	Edavanakkad	19 Feb 2014	13 Jun 2014	NA

No.	Name	Date	Dates	Period
8	Cheranalloor	6 Mar 2014	28 Aug 2014, 19 Mar 2015	Since November
9	Kuttampuzha	10 Feb 2014	30 Jun 2014	NA
	Thrissur district			
10	Erumapetty	30 Jun 2014	12 Jun 2014	June to September
11	Nattika	10 Feb 2014	2 Jul 2014, 30 Aug 2014, 25 Mar 2015	April to March
12	Puthur	28 Feb 2014	30 Jun 2014, 30 Aug 2014, 19 Jan 2015, 25 Mar 2015	July to September
	Kozhikode district			
13	Narippatta	13 Feb 2014	30 Jun 2014	June to September
14	Kadalundi	15 Feb 2014	30 Jun 2014, 19 Nov 2014	October to January
15	Unnikulam	6 May 2014	11 Jul 2014, 29 Dec 2014, 20 Feb 2015, 18 Mar 2015, 4 May 2015	Since May

implementation of some of the projects during the last quarter of the financial year (January–March 2015). Enormous delay in the preparation of the projects and getting approvals are the root causes of the poor plan performance of the GPs. A construction type project which is prepared by an assistant engineer in a GP has to be scrutinized and approved by an assistant executive engineer of a BP before its submission to the DPC. Similarly, technical sanction is also required from superior engineers for executing the construction-related projects. Due to these reasons, the execution starts during the second, third or fourth quarter of the financial year (Table 9.11).

Execution of Projects

The next stage is the execution stage. Here, the projects are entrusted to contractors or beneficiary committees for execution. Usually, more than one month is required for completing the procedure of tendering the work. The data given by the GPs reveal that except in a few GPs (4 GPs), the rest are executing majority of the projects through beneficiary committees and others (Table 9.12). The practice followed in the majority of the GPs is to entrust the execution of projects to beneficiary committees. Even road construction, tarring, construction of buildings, etc., are given to beneficiary committees without assessing their capability to execute the projects. The civil engineers of the GPs told us that they face serious problems in the execution of projects through beneficiary committees. Most of the beneficiary committees do not have expertise, skilled staff and equipment for undertaking road construction, repair, building construction and other civil works. In many cases, the beneficiary committee sublet the work to contractors and execute it. Second, settling the payments also involves difficulties due to the lack of production of proper receipts and other documents. Engineers told us that they also found it difficult to have an effective supervision of work executed by beneficiary committees. In majority of the cases, the quality of the work executed was also not up to the standard. The engineers are of the view that the execution of projects through the contractors is a better option for effecting speedy execution, ensuring quality of the work and fixing accountability of the work executed and effecting payments promptly.

Table 9.12 *No. of Projects Executed in 2014–2015 in GPs*

Sl No.	Name of GP	Contractor	Beneficiary Committee and Others	Total	Percentage Executed by Contractors
			Number of Projects Executed		
		Thiruvananthapuram district			
1	Kottukal	2	223	225	0.89
2	Anchuthengu	9	80	89	10.11
3	Vithura	17	153	170	10.00
		Kollam district			
4	Kottamkara	87	76	163	53.37
5	Kadakkal	122	144	266	45.86
6	Alappad	22	59	81	27.16
		Ernakulam district			
7	Edavanakkad	78	47	125	62.40
8	Cheranalloor	0	109	109	0.00
9	Kuttampuzha	23	243	266	8.65
		Thrissur district			
10	Erumapetty	10	123	133	7.5
11	Nattika	22	138	160	13.8
12	Puthur	113	119	232	48.7
		Kozhikode district			
13	Narippatta	45	108	153	29.41
14	Kadalundi	50	104	154	32.47
15	Unnikulam	10	291	301	3.32
	Total	**610**	**2,017**	**2,627**	**23.22**

Large and Unmanageable Number of Projects

A major reason for the poor execution of projects in the GPs is the large and unmanageable number of projects. The number of total projects in the GPs ranged between 81 and 301 (Table 9.12). The average number of projects, including spillover, executed in the GPs during the financial year 2014–2015 was 175. The data collected from the GPs suggest that one basic reason for the poor execution of projects is the large number of projects undertaken by the GPs. The representatives of GPs told us that the practice followed in almost all GPs is to divide the total annual plan amount among the ward members equally. The overall development requirement of the GP is seldom taken into consideration. The members are mostly concerned about the developmental activities in their wards, and distribution of benefits, subsidies, etc., to the people in the ward. The clashes between ruling and opposition members also prevent them from going for major development projects taking into consideration the overall development requirements of the GP. Due to the strong demands of ward members, GPs usually implement only very small or tiny projects.

The GPs reported that the engineering projects are prepared by the engineers of the GP. The rest are prepared by implementing officers of the GP and TIs. A serious issue raised by the engineers of the GP is that they find it difficult to prepare a large number of projects within a short period. They suggested that the same amount of work can be executed by reducing the number of projects by one-third or one-fourth. Taking into consideration the aforementioned facts, it is felt that it is necessary to reduce the number of projects in order to increase the efficiency of execution of projects.

In some of the GPs, an assistant engineer is in charge of more than one GP and finds it extremely difficult to attend to the project formulation and implementing activities in a satisfactory manner. Lack of sufficient number of overseers to supervise the execution of the work also affects the quality of the work. Among the 15 sample GPs, two GPs have no overseers and two GPs have one overseer each (Table 9.13). The rest of them have two overseers each. The engineers also pointed out that they do not get any clerical support for preparing the bills and other administrative work required for project formulation, execution and payment of bills. They demanded that at least one post of clerk should be created for the purpose.

Data are collected from the GPs about the total projects executed including the spillover projects and the number of projects completed

Table 9.13 *Strength of Engineering Staff in GPs*

| Sl No. | Name of GP | Strength of Engineering Staff | | | | Person Preparing the Project |
		AE	Overseer	Others	Total	
		Thiruvananthapuram district				
1	Kottukal	1	2	0	3	Officer of the GP
2	Anchuthengu	1	0	0	1	Officer of the GP & TI
3	Vithura	1	2	0	3	Officer of the GP
		Kollam district				
4	Kottamkara	1	2	0	3	Officer of the GP & TI
5	Kadakkal	1	2	1	4	Officer of the GP & TI
6	Alappad	1	3	1	5	Officer of the TI
		Ernakulam district				
7	Edavanakkad	1	2	0	3	Officer of the GP & TI
8	Cheranalloor	1	2	1	4	Officer of the TI
9	Kuttampuzha	1	2	0	3	Officer of the GP & TI
		Thrissur district				
10	Erumapetty	1	2	0	3	Officer of the GP & TI
11	Nattika	1	2	1	4	Officer of the GP
12	Puthur	1	1	1	3	Officer of the GP
		Kozhikode district				
13	Narippatta	1	2	0	3	Officer of the GP & TI
14	Kadalundi	1	1	1	3	Officer of the GP
15	Unnikulam	1	2	0	3	Officer of the GP & TI

Note: TI = Transferred institution

during the four financial years (Table 9.14). The data indicate that except in a few GPs, there has been a steady increase in the number of projects executed in all GPs. As the GPs are handling a large number of projects beyond their administrative capacity, the share of uncompleted projects is very high. Due to this, a good number of projects become spillover projects to be completed during the subsequent financial year. During the financial year 2014–2015, of the 15 GPs,

Table 9.14 *Details of Implementation of Projects in GPs*

Sl No.	Name of GP	Number of Projects Implemented			Percentage of Projects Completed			
		2011–2012	2012–2013	2013–2014	2014–2015	2011–2012	2012–2013	2013–2014	2014–2015
			Thiruvananthapuram district						
1	Kottukal	0	22	125	225	0	86.36	92.80	52.44
2	Anchuthengu	78	73	87	89	67.95	69.86	94.25	78.65
3	Vithura	0	149	156	170	0	85.23	85.90	71.18
			Kollam district						
4	Kottamkara	111	89	107	163	88.29	68.54	96.26	66.87
5	Kadakkal	171	158	235	266	57.89	48.10	74.04	71.80
6	Alappad	105	90	75	81	48.57	54.44	86.67	64.20
			Ernakulam district						
7	Edavanakkad	95	85	111	125	57.89	35.29	72.07	66.40
8	Cheranalloor	89	115	119	109	57.30	46.96	67.23	51.38
9	Kuttampuzha	183	214	191	266	61.75	77.57	73.30	59.40

								Thrissur district
10	Erumapetty	139	118	117	133	55.40	56.78	53.85	54.89
11	Nattika	0	84	114	160	0.00	91.67	80.70	83.13
12	Puthur	149	197	242	232	63.09	54.31	75.62	82.33
					Kozhikode district			
13	Narippatta	102	135	128	153	0.00	62.96	74.22	67.32
14	Kadalundi	0	121	129	154	0.00	54.55	79.84	47.40
15	Unnikulam	265	353	393	301	63.02	35.41	50.64	66.11
	Total	**1,487**	**2,003**	**2,329**	**2,627**	**57.70**	**57.91**	**73.38**	**65.85**

5 completed only less than 60 per cent of the number of projects executed. Another five GPs completed 60–70 per cent of the projects. This means that nearly 30 per cent to 40 per cent of the projects were not completed and became spillover projects.

Achievement of Financial Targets

The percentage of plan spending to total plan outlay gives an indication of achievement of financial targets. Here, the utilization of funds includes both plan and maintenance. Table 9.15 gives the percentage of fund utilization of the 15 sample GPs. During the financial year 2014–2015, only three GPs were able to spend about 75 per cent meant for plan and maintenance. Another seven GPs spent fund ranging between 60 and 72 per cent. The rest of them spent below 60 per cent of the funds. This indicates poor or unsatisfactory utilization of funds of the annual plan.

Bunching of expenditure to the last quarter or last month of a financial year is a common practice seen in the spending of GPs. In order to assess the pattern of plan spending, we have estimated the quarter-wise spending of the GPs for 2014–2015. Table 9.16 gives the quarter-wise plan spending of the GPs for 2014–2015.

During the first quarter of the financial year, of the 15 GPs, only two spent more than 10 per cent of their total expenditure. Of the 15 sample GPs, 8 had not spent a single rupee as plan expenditure during the first quarter of the fiscal year. In a majority of the GPs, spending starts only in the second quarter. Of the 15 GPs, nearly half spent a share between 10 and 22 per cent during the third quarter. Of the 15 GPs, two-thirds spent more than 50 per cent of the plan expenditure during the last quarter of the financial year. In three GPs, more than 73 per cent of the expenditure was incurred during the last quarter. Thus, spending the major share of plan expenditure during the last quarter of the financial year is the common practice of majority of GPs.

An attempt is also made to examine month-wise total plan and maintenance expenditure of the sample GPs (Table 9.17).

Table 9.15 *Percentage of Fund Utilization (Plan + Maintenance) in GPs*

Sl No.	Name of GP	2011–2012	2012–2013	2013–2014	2014–2015
		Thiruvananthapuram district			
1	Kottukal	0	65	60	65
2	Anchuthengu	38.6	59.85	74.2	69.7
3	Vithura	0	74.74	81	72.3
		Kollam district			
4	Kottamkara	69.6	59.2	69.54	48.08
5	Kadakkal	90	65	86	76
6	Alappad	47.18	42.81	81.4	66.17
		Ernakulam district			
7	Edavanakkad	75.2	49.7	78.5	69.5
8	Cheranalloor	80	55	75	70
9	Kuttampuzha	23.46	58.81	72.13	53.8
		Thrissur district			
10	Erumapetty	62.6	62.01	61.6	74.7
11	Nattika	0	75.47	79.68	75.35
12	Puthur	68.42	57.86	60.99	58.29
		Kozhikode district			
13	Narippatta	NA	NA	NA	NA
14	Kadalundi	39.5	54	69	54
15	Unnikulam	44.5	49.62	63.15	60.61
	Total	**44.89**	**50.65**	**68.58**	**66.49**

The GPs consider the first quarter as a period of plan formulation and getting approvals. The expenditure during the quarter is mainly related to the spillover projects (2.03%). Execution of works started during the second and third quarter and GPs starts spending money. But the LGs spend major share of plan expenditure during the last quarter.

In order to study the bunching of expenditure, we have also estimated the plan expenditure of the sample LGs during March 2015,

Table 9.16 Plan Spending: Quarter-Wise in 2014–2015 of GPs

Sl No.	Name of GP	Total Percentage				
		1st Quarter (April–June)	2nd Quarter (July–Sep)	3rd Quarter (Oct–Dec)	4th Quarter (Jan–March)	Total
		Thiruvananthapuram district				
1	Kottukal	0.00	27.79	31.09	41.13	100.00
2	Anchuthengu	1.71	16.91	28.39	52.99	100.00
3	Vithura	0.00	17.26	26.75	55.98	100.00
		Kollam district				
4	Kottamkara	0.00	11.27	11.56	77.17	100.00
5	Kadakkal	1.73	13.05	12.27	72.95	100.00
6	Alappad	0.15	28.07	20.49	51.28	100.00
		Ernakulam district				
7	Edavanakkad	1.54	25.57	29.74	43.16	100.00
8	Cheranalloor	0.00	4.81	50.98	44.21	100.00
9	Kuttampuzha	16.13	15.37	12.09	56.41	100.00

		Thrissur district			
10	Erumapetty	10.30	12.93	30.72	46.05	100.00
11	Nattika	0.00	23.42	18.72	57.86	100.00
12	Puthur	0.22	16.27	9.89	73.63	100.00
		Kozhikode district			
13	Narippatta	0.00	18.58	33.36	48.06	100.00
14	Kadalundi	0.00	12.83	30.53	56.64	100.00
15	Unnikulam	0.00	23.66	22.56	53.79	100.00
	Total	2.03	19.36	24.28	54.34	100.00

Table 9.17 *Total Plan Spending of the 15 GPs for 2014–2015 (Month-Wise)*

Month	Amount Spent (in ₹ lakh)	Percentage
Apr 2014	39.90	0.61
May 2014	5.72	0.09
Jun 2014	87.17	1.33
Jul 2014	288.60	4.41
Aug 2014	580.94	8.87
Sep 2014	398.07	6.08
Oct 2014	521.07	7.96
Nov 2014	516.30	7.88
Dec 2014	553.09	8.44
Jan 2015	429.90	6.56
Feb 2015	793.74	12.12
Mar 2015	2,335.42	35.66
Total	**6,549.92**	**100**

the last month of the financial year 2014–2015 (Table 9.18). It is interesting to note that two GPs spent more than half of the plan expenditure during the month of March 2015. Another two GPs spent 40 to 42 per cent of the plan expenditure during March 2015. Eight GPs spent 30 to 38 per cent of the plan expenditure during the month of March. Thus, bunching of plan expenditure during the last quarter or last month of the financial year is a common practice among GPs.

CONCLUSIONS

The earlier analysis may be concluded with the following observations: (a) the elaborate procedure followed for the appointment of plan coordinator, constitution of a number of working groups, conducting stakeholder consultations, discussion of project proposals in gram sabhas, finalization of status report and preparation of development plan and development seminar have not contributed much to the identification and preparation of projects. Lot of time and energy of

Table 9.18 *Plan Spending during March 2015*

Sl No.	Name of GP	Amount Spent in March (₹ Lakh)	Total for the Financial Year (Apr 2014 to Mar 2015)	Percentage of Plan Expenditure during March
		Thiruvananthapuram district		
1	Kottukal	388.36	1,363.74	28.48
2	Anchuthengu	115.63	285.66	40.48
3	Vithura	152.10	559.59	27.18
		Kollam district		
4	Kottamkara	180.25	310.61	58.03
5	Kadakkal	170.31	441.97	38.53
6	Alappad	87.24	267.44	32.62
		Ernakulam district		
7	Edavanakkad	68.59	235.42	29.14
8	Cheranalloor	62.12	184.99	33.58
9	Kuttampuzha	149.42	495.84	30.13
		Thrissur district		
10	Erumapetty	125.98	411.36	30.63
11	Nattika	125.27	347.41	36.06
12	Puthur	257.56	477.08	53.99
		Kozhikode district		
13	Narippatta	98.59	307.84	32.03
14	Kadalundi	170.65	460.41	37.06
15	Unnikulam	197.03	469.87	41.93

Source: Data Collected from GPs.

the LGs are spent for completing these procedures; (b) another issue is the use of a single plan guideline for different categories of LGs such as GPs, BPs, DPs, municipalities and MCs. Though the development requirement, nature and magnitude of plan activities, etc., are different among different categories of LG, a uniform guideline is used for all; (c) it is found that too much emphasis is given for completing a number of pre-project formulation procedures and too little emphasis for actual project formulation process; (d) as the peak period of plan formulation and implementation is a single period (between December and March) it results in poor plan formulation as well as execution; (e) lack of adequate time given for preparation of projects in the plan formulation guidelines (15 days in a year) results in preparation of poor projects; (f) an important reason for the poor plan performance at all levels—formulation, getting approvals, entrusting the work for execution and actual execution—is the large number of projects or unmanageable number of projects; (g) the practice of dividing annual plan fund ward-wise and preparing projects based on the interest of the ward member of GP is the reason for the large number of small and tiny projects; (h) due to the practice of having large number or excess number of projects, a substantial share of the projects remains incomplete during the end of the financial year; (i) due to the delays in project formulation, getting approvals from DPC, technical sanctions and awarding the work, the execution starts during the third or fourth quarter of the financial year resulting in poor execution and bunching of plan expenditure to the last quarter or last month of the financial year; (j) a reason for the poor execution and poor quality of projects is the practice of entrusting the execution of almost the entire projects (except a few) to beneficiary committees, who have no expertise, manpower, machinery or capacity to execute engineering projects; (k) the other reasons for poor plan performance are shortage of engineers, supporting field and clerical staff, restrictions imposed on the passing of bills by treasury, etc.

Decentralized Planning

10

Plan Performance of Municipal Corporations

INTRODUCTION

This chapter examines plan performance of MCs in Kerala. Kerala has six MCs. Of this, the Kannur municipality was upgraded as MC in November 2015. A review of the annual plan expenditure of municipalities and MCs in 2011–2015 indicated that the percentage of expenditure was very low in the case of MCs. This shows very poor plan performance of the MCs compared to municipalities. In this context, we attempt a study of the plan performance, namely plan formulation, execution and achievement of financial targets of MCs.

In Chapter 9, we have discussed objectives of decentralized planning, major issues, guidelines prescribed by the state government for various stages of plan formulation and execution, etc. The guidelines used for various stages of plan formulation and execution are presented in Tables 9.1–9.6. A uniform guideline is used for preparations of plans and executions in all categories of LGs, namely GPs, BPs, DPs, municipalities and MCs. Hence, the details of the guidelines are not presented in the chapter.

Annual Plan Expenditure of Urban LGs

The annual plan outlay and expenditure of the urban LGs, namely municipalities and MCs, for 2014–2015 is given in Table 10.1. Of the total plan outlay of ₹482 crore of municipalities, the actual plan expenditure was 40 per cent during the financial year 2014–2015. Compared to municipalities, the plan expenditure of MCs was very

Table 10.1 *Annual Plan Expenditure of Urban LGs 2014–2015*

LG	Outlay (₹ in Crore)	Expenditure (₹ in Crore)	% of Expenditure	Average Number of Projects Executed
Municipalities	482.38	191.12	40	208
MCs	376.05	114.85	31	1,051
Total	858.43	305.97	36	–

Source: State Finance Commission (2016).

low (31%). Attainment of very low plan utilization has been the basic problem of municipalities and MCs. A major reason for this was the execution of a large number of projects during a year. During 2014–2015, the average number of projects executed by municipalities and MCs was 208 and 1,051, respectively. In this context, we attempt an analysis of the plan performance of MCs based on a sample study.

Data Sources

Kerala has six MCs, namely Thiruvananthapuram, Kollam, Kochi, Thrissur, Kozhikode and Kannur. In this study, we have selected three MCs belonging to three regions of Kerala namely south, middle and north. The sample MCs are Thiruvananthapuram, Kochi and Kozhikode. Data were collected from them based on a detailed interview schedule. We also had detailed discussions with the officials and office-bearers responsible for the plan formulation and execution. The area, population, number of BPL households and average annual own resources of the MCs are given in Table 10.2. Among the sample MCs, Thiruvananthapuram MC was the largest in terms of area, number of wards and population. Kozhikode ranks second and Kochi, third.

Plan Formulation Stage

Ineffective Working Groups

We have already presented the guideline on plan formulation, approvals and execution in Chapter 9. The first step in plan formulation is appointment of plan coordinator, constitution of working groups,

Table 10.2 *Area and Population of Sample MCs*

Sl No.	Name of MC	Number of Wards	Area (in Sq. Km)	Population (Number)	Number of BPL Households	Average Own Resources in ₹ Lakh
1	Thiruvananthapuram	100'	215.86	966,856	61,845	8,853.25
2	Kochi	74	94.88	602,046	63,568	9,042.61
3	Kozhikode	75	118.59	608,503	27,602	4,876.84

Source: Data collected from MCs.

conducting stakeholder consultations, convening ward sabhas, preparation of draft development plan and organizing development seminars. As per the guidelines issued by the state government, the entire procedure should be completed within the month of November and December for the annual plan starting from April of the next financial year. Table 10.3 gives the date of appointment of plan coordinator, number of working groups, date of meeting of the working groups, date of SHM, number of participants, date of ward sabha meetings and development seminar. The plan coordinators were appointed between December and January in the sample MCs. The number of working groups constituted ranged from 15 to 19. Though the plan guidelines

Table 10.3 *Plan Formulation Process in 2014–2015*

Sl No.	Item	Thiruvananthapuram	Kochi	Kozhikode
1	Date of appointment of plan coordinator	1 Jan 2014	7 Dec 2013	28 Jan 2014
2	No. of working groups	19	17	15
3	Date of working groups meeting	6 Jan 2014	28 Jan 2014 3 Feb 2014 30 Apr 2014	25 Jan 2014
4	Date of SHM	23 Jan 2014	28 Jan 2014	8 Aug 2012
5	No. of persons participated (SHM)	141	113	17
6	Ward sabha meeting (month)	Jan 2014	Jan 2014	Jan 2014
7	Average no. of participants	237	71	80
8	Date of development seminar	4 Feb 2014	3 Feb 2014	6 Feb 2014
9	No. of participants	1,635	473	354

Source: Data collected from MCs.

suggest 17 working groups, Thiruvananthapuram MC constituted 19 working groups. Kochi and Kozhikode had 17 and 15 working groups, respectively. It is reported by the MCs that working groups had met mostly during January and February 2014. Of the three MCs, all of them have conducted SHM. Among the MCs, the participation in SHM was very poor in Kozhikode. It was found that the role of the working group in the plan formulation process was relatively insignificant. In Thiruvananthapuram and Kozhikode MCs, they met only once. In Kochi, the working group met thrice. It seems that the MCs constituted the working groups simply to satisfy the formalities of plan formulation. Our discussion with the officials of the MCs revealed that the working groups had not contributed much in project preparation and providing inputs for project formulation. The MCs conducted one meeting with the stakeholders, but the number of participants was very low in Kozhikode MC.

Ward Sabhas and Development Seminar

All the MCs conducted ward sabha meeting consisting of the voters belonging to each ward of the MCs. The MCs reported that the ward sabhas were convened exclusively to discuss the annual plans. The average number of participants in the ward sabhas ranged between 71 and 80 in 2 MCs and 237 in 1 MC. The officials of the MCs pointed out that the voters are not interested to participate in the ward sabha meetings. Most of the participants in ward sabha meetings are persons such as Kudumbashree workers, beneficiaries of housing and other schemes, the casual workers employed for cleaning work, etc. It is pointed out that majority of the participants were women. Other category of people like retired people, teachers, residents associations office-bearers, etc., attending the ward sabhas were few in number. Due to this, serious discussion about the development issues, needs, type of projects required, etc., are not taking place. Development seminar is visualized as a meeting place to discuss the overall development issues and plan projects of MCs. As it is a big meeting of mostly local political leaders and their followers, no serious discussions are taking place. Major part of the meeting is devoted for inaugural function speeches of local political leaders and other items. The MCs opined that a lot of time and resources are being spent for completing the earlier procedure in the first stage of plan formulation. It is also pointed out that the MCs are not getting much benefit from the earlier exercise in identifying development issues, projects and formulating project proposals. Thus, we have to conclude that the elaborate exercise conducted to satisfy the norms of plan formulation does not provide much inputs for project identification and preparation.

Preparation and Approval of Projects

The second step in plan formulation process is preparation of projects. According to the guidelines of plan formulation, the MCs have to prepare the entire projects of an annual plan between 15 December and 10 January. A serious error in the plan guideline is the short period given for preparation of a large number of projects. Due to this, no MC was able to prepare projects within the stipulated time. The annual plan consisting of a large number of projects and schemes was approved by the MCs between February and August (Table 10.4).

Table 10.4 *Approval of Projects and Annual Plan of 2014–2015 in MCs*

Sl No.	Items	Thiruvananthapuram	Kochi	Kozhikode
1	Date of approval of annual plan by MC council	11 Aug 2014	11 Jul 2014	27 Feb 2014
2	Date of approval by DPC	22 Aug 2014	17 Jul 2014	31 Jul 2014
3	Months in which execution of project started	NA	Jul 2014 to Jan 2015	Jul 2014
4	Total no. of projects	1,161	825	678
5	Projects executed by contractors	NA	793	84
6	Percentage executed by contractors	NA	96.12	12.39

Source: Data collected from MCs.

Kozhikode MC approved the plan on 27 February 2014. While in other MCs, namely Kochi and Thiruvananthapuram, the date of approval was 11 July and 11 August 2014, respectively. The DPC gave the approval of the annual plan in July and August. In the case of a number of projects, the detailed projects are prepared only after the approval of the annual plan by the DPC.

Issue of Technical Sanction

Besides this, technical sanction from the competent authority is required for implementing the projects. The projects, especially engineering type of projects, are prepared by the engineers of the MC. In all the MCs, the engineering wing is headed by the rank of a superintending engineer. Hence, for scrutiny and approval, the construction projects should be sent to the chief engineer, LSGD. Similarly, the technical sanction for execution will have to be accorded by the chief engineer, LSGD. For getting these approvals, a lot of time is required. Hence, the actual execution of projects started only in July, that is, from the second quarter of the financial year. In Kochi MC, it was reported that the execution of a good number of projects were started since January 2015, the last quarter of the financial year. We do not know the position of Thiruvananthapuram MC, since they have not provided the information.

Large and Unmanageable Number of Projects

A major issue in the annual plan of MCs is the formulation and execution of a large number of projects, which is beyond the administrative capacity of an MC. During the year 2014–2015, the number of projects implemented in the sample MCs ranged between 678 and 1,161 (Table 10.5). Instead of having medium type projects, the MC formulates large number of small, very small and tiny projects. The general practice followed in MCs is to share the total plan outlay wardwise. The councillors want to have a large number of small projects and are not interested to have medium or bigger projects. Here, the concept is to give emphasis on ward-level activities and ignoring the overall development requirement of the MC. The projects are prepared

Table 10.5 *Number of Projects Implemented and Completed*

		2012–2013	2013–2014	2014–2015
I	**Thiruvananthapuram**			
1.	Number of projects implemented	971	998	1,161
2.	Number of projects completed	201	387	258
3.	Percentage of completion	20.70	38.78	22.23
II	**Kochi**			
1.	Number of projects implemented	621	816	825
2.	Number of projects completed	243	488	552
3.	Percentage of completion	39.13	59.80	66.91
III	**Kozhikode**			
1.	Number of projects implemented	445	555	678
2.	Number of projects completed	267	322	401
3.	Percentage of completion	60.00	58.02	59.14

Source: Data collected from MCs.

by the officers and engineers of the MC as well as those belonging to TIs. As the MC has to prepare a large number of projects with limited staff, there is also delay in project formulation.

Execution of Projects

We have examined the number of projects implemented, the number of projects that have completed the execution and percentage of completion to total projects of the sample MCs for three years. Table 10.5 gives the details of projects implemented and completed during three years. Thiruvananthapuram MC has been implementing a large number of projects beyond their administrative capacity. As a result, they were able to complete only a portion of the projects and rest of them became spillover projects. During the year 2012–2013, only 21 per cent of the projects were completed. The completion rate was 39 per cent in 2013–2014 and 22 per cent in 2014–2015. The large and unmanageable number of projects is the root cause for the poor plan performance and low plan expenditure.

In Kochi MC, the situation is not different. The MC has been implementing a large number of projects beyond their administrative capacity. The completion rate of the projects was also poor. But compared to other sample MCs, Kochi achieved a higher completion rate in 2014–2015. Kozhikode MC had a lower number of projects compared to other MCs, but the completion rate was below 60 per cent. Thus, the evidence suggests that all the three sample MCs have been implementing a large number of projects beyond their administrative capacity resulting in high rate of non-completed projects or spillover projects.

Achievement of Financial Targets

Percentage of plan expenditure to the total outlay can be taken as an indicator of the achievement of financial targets. Table 10.6 gives the percentage of plan expenditure to total outlay for three years from 2012–2013 to 2014–2015.

In Thiruvananthapuram MC, there has been a steady decline in the percentage of plan expenditure. It fell from 75 per cent in 2012–2013 to 46 per cent in 2014–2015. In Kochi MC, the percentage of plan utilization maintained almost a steady level and ranged between 60 per cent and 68 per cent during the three years. The situation is no better in Kozhikode MC. The percentage of plan expenditure ranged between 45 per cent and 52 per cent during the three years. These figures indicate a dismal picture about the financial achievement of plan targets. The core issues in the execution of projects of MCs are to

Table 10.6 *Percentage of Fund Utilization (Plan+Maintenance) to Plan Outlay in MCs*

Sl No.	Name of MC	2012–2013	2013–2014	2014–2015
1	Thiruvananthapuram	75.52	64.88	45.62
2	Kochi	60.54	67.58	67.67
3	Kozhikode	47.00	45.00	52.00

Source: Data collected from MCs.

increase the percentage of plan utilization and to achieve 100 per cent of financial targets.

Bunching of Plan Expenditure

An unhealthy practice of plan spending in MCs is the bunching of expenditure towards the last quarter or the last month of the financial year. In order to examine this aspect, we have collected data on the quarter-wise plan spending. Table 10.7 gives the quarter-wise share of total expenditure. In the MCs, the plan spending in the first quarter was very small or nil. During the first quarter of the financial year 2014–2015, Thiruvananthapuram MC spent 3.2 per cent and Kochi MC 4 per cent of total expenditure. Kozhikode MC had not spent a single rupee.

There is some progress in the plan spending during the second quarter and the spending ranges to about 11 per cent of the total expenditure. Nearly one-fourth of the spending of MCs was done during the third quarter of the financial year. It is likely that the expenditure shown in the first three quarters is mainly that of spill-over projects of the previous years. The quarter-wise spending of MCs shows that 59 to 66 per cent of the total expenditure was spent during the last quarter of the financial year. Bunching of expenditure to the last quarter or last month of the financial year indicates hasty spending.

Month-Wise Plan Expenditure

We have also attempted an examination of month-wise plan spending of the MCs for 2014–2015 (Table 10.8). A trend noticed in all the three MCs is that the plan expenditure is very meagre or nil in the first three months. The second quarter also witnessed very small share of plan expenditure. The MCs spent a share of 22 to 27 per cent of the plan expenditure in the third quarter. Bunching the plan expenditure to the last quarter, especially to the last two months, is the common trend observed. All the three MCs in our study spent major share of their plan spending in the last two months of the financial

Table 10.7 *Plan Expenditure of MCs: Quarter-Wise in 2014–2015*

Sl No.	Name of MC	1st Quarter (April–June)	2nd Quarter (July–Sep)	3rd Quarter (Oct–Dec)	4th Quarter (Jan–March)	Total
		Amount Spent (₹ lakhs)				
1	Thiruvananthapuram	365.95	1,264.99	2,569.65	7,382.07	11,582.68
2	Kochi	412.52	1,096.88	2,706.95	5,995.23	10,211.59
3	Kozhikode	0	905.52	1,883.46	5,319.27	8,108.26
	Total	**778.47**	**3,267.40**	**7,160.07**	**18,696.59**	**29,902.53**
		Percentage				
1	Thiruvananthapuram	3.16	10.92	22.19	63.73	100
2	Kochi	4.04	10.74	26.51	58.71	100
3	Kozhikode	0.00	11.17	23.23	65.60	100
	Total	**2.60**	**10.93**	**23.94**	**62.53**	**100**

Source: Data collected from MCs.

Table 10.8 *Total Plan Spending of MCs for 2014–2015*

Month	Amount Spent (in Lakh)				Percentage			
	Thiruvananthapuram	Kochi	Kozhikode		Thiruvananthapuram	Kochi	Kozhikode	
Apr 2014	0	0	0		0.00	0.00	0.00	
May 2014	365.95	0	0		3.16	0.00	0.00	
Jun 2014	0	412.52	0		0.00	4.04	0.00	
Jul 2014	297.00	388.54	140.17		2.56	3.80	1.73	
Aug 2014	696.44	434.76	543.43		6.01	4.26	6.70	
Sep 2014	271.54	273.57	221.90		2.34	2.68	2.74	
Oct 2014	781.08	529.04	541.73		6.74	5.18	6.68	
Nov 2014	618.74	1,136.17	374.15		5.34	11.13	4.61	
Dec 2014	1,169.82	1,041.73	967.57		10.10	10.20	11.93	
Jan 2015	788.87	562.04	355.74		6.81	5.50	4.39	
Feb 2015	1,354.81	895.42	923.68		11.70	8.77	11.39	
Mar 2015	5,238.38	4,537.76	4,039.84		45.24	44.44	49.83	
Total	**11,582.68**	**10,211.59**	**8,108.26**		**100.00**	**100**	**100**	**100**

Source: Data collected from MCs.

year. Thiruvananthapuram MC spends 57 per cent, Kochi MC spends 53 per cent and Kozhikode MC 61 per cent of the plan expenditure during the last two months of the financial year. The three MCs spent an amount of 44 to 50 per cent of the plan expenditure during March 2015, the last month of the financial year 2014–2015. For achieving fiscally sound spending, there is a need to reverse the spending pattern for plan purposes.

CONCLUSIONS

The assessment of the plan performance of MCs may be concluded as follows: (a) the plan formulation and execution guidelines which are meant for three-tier panchayats are not suitable to urban conditions and urban LGs. An unsuitable and uniform guideline is used for urban LGs; (b) the elaborate procedures followed for the appointment of plan coordinator, constitution of working groups, etc., have not contributed much to preparation of projects or annual plan; (c) MCs spent major part of their effort and time for completing the elaborate and irrelevant procedure at the pre-project preparation stage and neglected project preparation and execution; (d) though the ward sabhas are assigned a key role in the formulation of development plan, they have not contributed much to identify development needs, projects and giving suggestions for the local-level development. Majority of the participants in ward sabhas were Kudumbashree workers, beneficiaries of housing and other schemes and workers employed for cleaning works of the MCs, etc., (e) the major cause for the poor plan performance is the implementation of a large and unmanageable number of projects, resulting in non-completion of a sizeable share of projects; (f) total annual plan amount of an MC is divided among ward councillors and projects are prepared to satisfy the ward and thereby pushing political interests at the cost of the overall development of MC; (g) low priority is given to actual preparation of projects and they are hastily formulated and executed during the last quarter or last month of the financial year; (h) in spite of the experience of MCs for implementing annual plans for more than two decades, the practice of bunching of plan expenditure to the last quarter or last month of the financial year continues; (i) for improving the plan performance, a thorough revision of the plan guidelines, cut in irrelevant procedures at pre-project formulation stage, reduction in the number of projects to manageable limits, preparation of projects based on overall development of the MCs, change in the procedure of approval, sanctions, etc., and time-bound and target-orientated implementation are needed.

Summary and Lessons from Kerala's Fiscal Decentralization

SUMMARY AND CONCLUSION

The objective of the study is to examine two decades of fiscal decentralization experience in Kerala. It examines the mobilization of own sources of revenue, finances of GPs, BPs and DPs, finances of municipalities, intergovernmental fiscal transfers through SFC, devolution recommendations of the 5th SFC and status of implementation, assessment of decentralized planning of GPs and MCs.

The analysis of fiscal decentralization on the aspect of own sources of revenue of LGs arrived at the following conclusions. The fiscal decentralization that was implemented in Kerala is partial or limited; (a) in spite of assignment of a number of additional functions and expenditure responsibilities to LGs, no new tax or non-tax items were transferred to LGs; (b) the successive state governments in Kerala have not taken steps to revise rate of taxes or fees periodically. Efforts were not made to make appropriate changes in the provisions of Acts or rules for the purpose; (c) the LGs were not given powers to revise the rate of taxes and non-tax items and effect periodical revision. The power to revise the rate revision was retained by the state government; (d) the state policy of neglecting own resource mobilization of LGs and providing funds through devolution and transfer have increased the dependence of LGs on transferred resources; (e) the GPs, municipalities and MCs also give low priority for collection of tax and non-tax revenue and expanding tax base. All the earlier factors have contributed to a deterioration in the own resource mobilization of GPs, municipalities and MCs.

The central issue in the finances of GPs is the very low share of its own resources and heavy reliance on funds from the state government for its functioning. The state government, which retained powers to revise taxes and non-taxes of LGs, had not taken steps to effect periodical revision for about two decades. In the case of property tax, which accounts for major share of tax revenue of the GPs, the rate of tax was revised after a gap of 17 years. But the rate revision was practically withdrawn after two years. In the case of professional tax, which account for one-third of total tax revenue of GPs, the upper ceiling limit of the tax rate remained unchanged for the last 31 years (since 1988) due to inaction of the successive central governments. As per KPRA, 1994, the core functions of GPs are mandatory, civic and development. But a review of the structure of expenditure shows that the largest share of expenditure was incurred on its agency functions such as distribution of welfare pensions, implementation of MGNREGS and other CSS. This has created a situation in which the GPs spend major share of their effort, time and manpower for non-priority agency functions neglecting core functions.

The analysis of the finances of BPs and DPs may be concluded as follows. The functions, responsibilities and resources assigned to BPs are much different from that of GPs. They are not assigned mandatory, and civic functions or collection of taxes. BPs are entrusted with functions related to development plans (annual plan), maintenance of own assets and assets of TIs, coordination of the activities of TIs, implementation of CSS, etc. For meeting the expenses relating to establishment, administration, maintenance and annual plan, they solely depend on the transfer of funds from the state government. The policy of transferring the financial burden of some schemes to BPs by the state government and asking them to pay from the development fund or through borrowing have adversely affected the implementation of annual plans and created severe fiscal problems.

The functions assigned to the DPs are similar to that of BPs. The main source of receipts of the DPs are devolved funds from the state government. It ranged between 91 and 97 per cent of the total receipts. Formulation and implementation of annual plans and maintenance of road and non-road assets are the main activities of the DPs. A disturbing and unhealthy change that had been taking place in plan spending was a shift of allocation of resources from productive sector to service sector. In the case of utilization of maintenance fund, the DPs give high priority for roads compared to non-road assets.

Though additional expenditure responsibilities are assigned to municipalities, they were not given new tax or non-tax items or to effect periodical revision of its rates. Though there is considerable scope for increasing their tax and non-tax revenue, through periodical revision, they could not implement it due to lack of powers. A review of the structure of expenditure shows that annual plan accounts for the largest share followed by establishment, maintenance, welfare pensions and CSS. Payment of pensions to retired municipal staff by municipalities has become a serious fiscal problem due to collapse of the arrangement of pension payment by state government and municipalities. Entrusting additional agency functions like distribution of social welfare pension and implementation of CSS have adversely affected the execution of their civic functions like waste disposal, waste water disposal, containing stray dog menace, running slaughter houses, public toilets, etc.

Sound intergovernmental fiscal transfer through appropriate institutions is the cornerstone of fiscal decentralization. Kerala's experience of fiscal transfers through SFCs gives a mixed picture of merits as well as demerits. In other words, Kerala's achievement with regard to fiscal decentralization is partial. The merits are timely constitution of SFCs, devolution of state resources based on clear fiscal norms, earmarking a share of the annual plan outlay to LGs, transferring sufficient funds, devolution of funds for three purposes, namely general purpose, maintenance and development, etc. The demerits are delays in implementation of two SFC reports for five years, implementation of a small share of recommendations of the SFCs, non-implementation of recommendations other than devolution, dual practice of accepting a large number of SFC recommendations and not implementing most of them, undesirable role of the finance department in implementations of the SFC reports bypassing the role of LSGD in SFC reports, etc.

The 5th SFC's approach to devolution is much different from the approaches followed by the earlier SFCs. In place of devolution based on $(t-2)$ or $(t-3)$ method, the Commission used t method for devolving state taxes based on the year of devolution. Instead of giving maintenance fund based on unreliable data, the Commission decided to distribute the maintenance fund to each LG on the basis of the actual road and non-road assets. Regarding the practice of giving a share of the annual plan size of Kerala as development fund, the Commission recommended to give a share of net proceeds of SOTR as development fund. The 5th SFC wanted to treat the grants of 14th UFC given to LGs as a separate grant and it should be transferred to LGs in addition to SFC's devolution. The Commission also recommended that the award is to be given specifying the amount of money to be devolved to each LG for each year of the award period. But the state government delayed the implementation of the 5th SFC reports for two years, rejected most of the devolution recommendations, devolved funds in an arbitrary manner, transferred a lower amount to LGs compared to 5th SFC recommendations denied the constitutional right of LGs to get funds as per SFCs and subverted the fiscal decentralization process.

An assessment of the decentralized planning in GPs arrived at the following conclusions. The elaborate procedure followed for the appointment of plan coordinator, constitution of a number of working groups, conducting stakeholder consultations, discussion of project proposals in gram sabhas, finalization of status report, preparation of development plan and development seminar have not contributed much to the identification and preparation of projects. Lot of time and energy of the LGs are spent for completing these procedures. The other reasons for poor plan performance are as follows. A uniform plan guideline for all categories of rural and urban LGs, too little emphasis for preparing sound projects, formulation and implementation of projects during the peak period (between December and March), lack of adequate time for project preparation, formulation of a very large number of projects or unmanageable number of projects, division of total annual plan fund ward-wise, execution of projects during the last quarter of the financial year, bunching of plan expenditure to the last quarter or last month, poor execution of projects by beneficiary committees, shortage of engineering staff, restrictions imposed on passing bills of the completed projects in treasury, etc.

The plan performance of MCs are much worse than the GPs. It is disturbing to note that the annual plan and maintenance expenditure of Thiruvananthapuram MC was 45.6 per cent, Kochi MC 67.6 per cent and Kozhikode MC 52 per cent of annual plan outlay in 2014–2015. The causes for the poor plan performance of MCs are similar to that of GPs.

The analysis in the previous chapters based on the fiscal data collected from the sample LGs and the summary and conclusions presented earlier support the hypotheses we put forward to explain the fiscal decentralization experience in Kerala. The hypotheses which are supported by empirical evidence are presented here.

Partial and Distorted Fiscal Decentralization

The outcome of fiscal decentralization in Kerala is poor or unsatisfactory due to partial and distorted implementation of fiscal decentralization with regard to transfer of taxes and non-tax items, revision of the rate of tax and non-tax, implementation of SFC recommendations, dual control of TIs and staff, interference in administration through a host of regulations and controls and entrusting additional agency functions without expansion of administrative machinery and staff.

Lack of Freedom to Mobilize Own Resources

The fiscal policy of non-transfer of new taxes to LGs, non-transfer of powers to revise rates or effect periodical revision of tax and non-tax items; failure of successive state governments to effect periodical revision of rates of taxes and non-tax items collected by the LGs and low priority given by the LGs for own resource mobilization have contributed to poor own resource mobilization and heavy reliance on transferred funds by the LGs.

Growth of Agency Functions at the Cost of Civic Functions

Though core functions of GPs, municipalities and MCs are mandatory, civic and development, the assignment of additional agency functions like distribution of welfare pensions, implementation of CSS, etc., without expanding the administrative machinery and staff, have resulted in the deterioration of its civic functions like waste disposal, controlling stray dogs, running slaughter houses, etc., and plan performance of development plans.

Fiscal Transfers through SFCs

Though Kerala's fiscal transfers through SFCs has certain merits, namely timely constitution, fiscal devolution based on norms, somewhat sufficient transfer of funds to meet their functions; the demerits, such as delayed implementation of SFC reports, implementation of a small share of recommendations, non-implementation of most of the recommendations other than devolution and refusing to implement the accepted recommendations, under some pretext, outweigh the merits.

Poor Performance of Development Plans

The causes for the poor plan performance of urban and rural LGs can be attributed to factors such as irrational and irrelevant plan formulation guidelines giving too much emphasis for pre-project preparation formalities, an unsuitable and uniform plan guidelines meant for all categories of LGs, non-functioning working groups, low priority and very little time given for actual project preparations, implementation of a large and unmanageable number of projects, splitting projects into tiny projects giving undue importance to wards, delays in getting approvals and entrusting work, entrusting execution of majority of projects to incompetent beneficiary committees, inadequate number of engineers and supporting staff, delayed execution of projects, bunching of plan expenditure to last quarter or the last month and restrictions imposed on passing bills due to treasury restrictions.

LESSONS FROM KERALA'S FISCAL DECENTRALIZATION

Transfer of Functions to GPs and Municipalities

Kerala has transferred a large number of functions coming under the category of mandatory, civic, general and sector-wise. The sector-wise responsibilities are agriculture, animal husbandry, minor irrigation, fisheries, housing, water supply, electricity, education, public health, social welfare, poverty alleviation, SC/ST development, etc. A few institutions belonging to the departments of agriculture, animal husbandry, health services, general education, etc., are also transferred to them. Transfer of a large number of functions to the GPs and municipalities without considering the size of administrative set-up, staff, fiscal powers, availability of resources, etc., have resulted in overburden of their activities and poor performance on all fronts.

The lessons from Kerala's decentralization and fiscal decentralization experience suggest that transfer of a few important functions which are relevant to GPs and municipalities and which can be executed efficiently with the small administrative set-up, staff, resources, powers, etc., are desirable to be transferred to GPs and municipalities. Transferring a large number of functions at the early stage of decentralization will result in poor execution of these

Dual Control of Transferred Institutions by LGs and the State Government

The state government has transferred a few institutions to GPs and municipalities and assigned a few functions to them. The major institutions transferred to GPs are krishi bhavans, veterinary dispensaries, primary health centres, government dispensaries and government lower primary schools. Most of the powers relating to administration, staff, activities, etc., of the institutions are retained by the state government. The GPs and municipalities are assigned the role of maintaining and repairing the assets and providing funds for its day-to-day activities. A system of dual control by the LGs and the state government is implemented. This dual control has created confusion in terms of the powers on administration, control over staff and other aspects of the working of the institutions. Conflicts between LGs and the TIs on the issue of dual control has become a common thing.

The lessons we learned from this is that dual control is not a sound mechanism for the efficient functioning of the institutions. It is better to give full authority and powers to administer a primary health centre, government dispensary and veterinary dispensary to GPs and municipalities. The current practice of entrusting the repairs and maintenance of a government institution to LGs is not a desirable thing. LGs are a tier of government in a federal country and it should be treated as a government.

Low Priority and Poor Execution of Civic Functions

According to the KPRA, 1994, and the KMA, 1994, the basic functions of GPs and municipalities are to execute civic functions which are directly related to the public health and welfare of the people. The important civic functions are collection and disposal of solid waste, regulation of liquid waste disposal, maintenance of environmental hygiene, vector control, regulation of slaughtering of animals, street lighting, adoption of programmes of immunization, prevention and control of diseases, establishment of burning and burial grounds, provision of parking places for vehicles, construction of waiting sheds, public toilets and bathing ghat and control of stray dogs. But currently the LGs are treating these as unimportant or low priority functions. They say that they have to execute a large number of other functions such as maintenance of assets of TIs, formulation and execution of annual plans, agency functions such as distribution of social welfare pensions and execution of CSS.

The lessons we learned is that in the context of decentralization and transfer of more functions, LGs accord low priority to their core civic functions and give high priority to agency functions, maintenance of assets, etc. This is not the mandate of the GPs and municipalities. Instead of the current practice of giving low priority to civic functions, the LGs should give top priority for it.

Agency Functions and Its Negative Effects

The assignment of agency functions such as distribution of welfare pensions, implementation of MGNREGA and other schemes have adversely affected the execution of their mandatory, civic and developmental functions of the GPs, municipalities and MCs. The distribution of social welfare pensions done by the government departments were transferred to the GPs and municipalities since 1996. The distribution of pension having a large number of beneficiaries was done manually by the LGs resulting in substantial increase in the administrative work. Studies suggest that transfer of pension distribution without corresponding increase in administrative set-up and staff had affected all aspects of the functioning of GPs. Though there has been substantial increase in workload of GPs between 1995 and 2005, the average number of staff increased from 12.5 in 1995 to 14.9 in 2005 per GP. Studies suggest that the GPs were forced to stop their office work for many days for distribution of welfare pensions. Similarly, implementation of MGNREGA and diversion of staff for it has adversely affected other activities of the GPs.

The lessons we learned is that transfer of new agency functions involving a lot of administrative work have adversely affected all activities of the GPs and municipalities. For efficient implementation of mandatory, civic and development functions, it is not advisable to take up low priority agency functions. It is better to entrust these agency functions to other agencies.

Partial Fiscal Decentralization

The outcome of fiscal decentralization in Kerala is poor or unsatisfactory due to partial and distorted implementation of fiscal decentralization with regard to transfer of taxes and non-tax items, revision of the rate of tax and non-tax, implementation of SFC recommendations, dual control of TIs and staff, and interference in administration through a host of regulations and controls.

Kerala's experience suggests that partial and distorted fiscal decentralization won't give better performance. To achieve better results, service delivery, increasing social welfare and accelerating the local-level development, one has to opt for a full-scale fiscal decentralization system based on four pillars, namely expenditure assignment, revenue assignment, sound intergovernmental transfers and sub-national borrowing.

Lack of Freedom to Mobilize Own Resources

The preconditions for sound fiscal decentralization are allocation of own sources of revenue to LGs and giving full freedom to levy, collect and revise rate of taxes and non-tax items. But the policy pursued by successive governments in Kerala has been non-transfer of new taxes to LGs, and non-transfer of powers to revise rates or effect periodical revision, thereby curtailing LGs freedom to mobilize own resources. This has contributed to poor own resources mobilization and heavy reliance on transferred funds by the LGs.

The lessons we learned from this experience are that LGs should be given full freedom to levy, collect and effect periodical revision of the rate of tax and non-tax items. For reducing the dependence on tied transferred funds and, to become more autonomous, the LGs should focus on the mobilization of their own resources.

Poor Implementation of SFC Recommendations

Though Kerala's fiscal transfers through SFCs have certain merits, namely timely constitution, fiscal devolution based on norms, some-what sufficient transfer of funds to meet their functions; the demerits outweigh the merits. The demerits are delayed implementation of SFC reports, implementation of a small share of recommendations, non-implementation of most of the recommendations other than devolution, refusing to implement majority of the accepted recom-mendations, etc. Poor implementation of SFC recommendations is the most serious issue in Kerala's intergovernmental fiscal transfers.

The paradox of Kerala's intergovernmental fiscal transfers is timely constitution of SFCs on the one hand and poor implementation of SFC recommendations on the other. In this context, for achieving sound fiscal decentralization, one has to give equal weightage for timely constitution as well as prompt implementation of SFC's recommendations.

Poor Performance of Decentralized Plan

Poor plan formulation and execution are the major issues of development plans of the LGs in Kerala. It can be attributed to factors such as irrational and irrelevant plan formulation guidelines giving too much emphasis for pre-project preparation formalities, unsuitable and uniform plan guidelines meant for all categories of LGs, non-functioning working groups, low priority and very little time given for actual project preparations, implementation of a large and unmanageable number of projects, splitting projects into tiny projects giving undue importance to wards, delays in getting approvals and entrusting work, entrusting execution of majority of projects to incompetent beneficiary committees, inadequate number of engineers and supporting staff, delayed execution of projects, bunching of plan expenditure to the last quarter or last month and restrictions imposed on passing bills due to treasury restrictions.

Kerala's decentralized planning experience indicates the following: (a) lack of freedom to the LGs for plan formulation based on their requirements, priorities, geographic conditions, etc., (b) the plans are centralized type based on the plan objectives and plan guidelines of the state government; (c) in this context, the important issue is transforming the centralized planning to a decentralized one; (d) for transforming it to decentralized one and making it more efficient, the following changes are needed: (i) discard the rotten plan guidelines, (ii) give freedom to the LGs to prepare a plan based on their needs and priorities, (iii) preparation of projects based on development requirements of the LGs, (iv) reduce the number of projects by combining small projects coming under one category and (v) time-bound execution and entrusting work to competent contractors.

BIBLIOGRAPHY

Alok, V. N. 2006. 'Local Government Organisation and Finance'. In *Local Governance in Developing Countries* (pp. 205–231), edited by Anwar Shah. Washington, DC: World Bank.

Bahl, Roy, and Jorge-Martinez Vazquez. 2005. *Sequencing Fiscal Decentralisation*. Atlanta, GA: Andrew Young School of Policy Studies, Georgia State University.

Bird, Richard M. 2000. *Intergovernmental Fiscal Relations: Universal Principles, Local Applications*. Working Paper 00–02. Atlanta, GA: Andrew Young School of Policy Studies, Georgia State University.

Bird, Richard M., Robert D. Ebel, and Christian L. Wallice, ed. 1995. *Decentralisation of the Socialist State, Intergovernmental Finance in Transition Economies: Regional and Sectoral Studies*. Washington, DC: World Bank.

Centre for Development Studies. 2001. *Kerala Research Programme on Local Level Development*. Report 5, 2000–2001. Thiruvananthapuram: CDS.

Charvak. 2000. *From Decentralisation of Planning to People's Planning: Experiences of the Indian States of West Bengal and Kerala*. Thiruvananthapuram: Centre for Development Studies.

Chathukulam, Jos, and M. S. John. 2002. 'Five Years of Participatory Planning in Kerala: Rhetoric and Reality'. *Economic & Political Weekly* 37 (49): 4917–4926.

Fukasaku, Kiichiro, and Luiz R. de Mello Jr. 1997. *Fiscal Decentralisation and Macroeconomic Stability: The Experience of Large Developing and Transition Economies*. Paris: Organisation of Economic Cooperation and Development.

Government of Kerala. 2011. *Action Taken Report on First Part of the Report of 4th SFC*. Thiruvananthapuram: GoK.

———. 2012. *Action Taken Report of Part II Report of the 4th SFC*. Thiruvananthapuram: GoK.

———. 2016. *Annual Plan Review 2014–15*. Thiruvananthapuram: Planning and Economic Affairs Department.

———. 2018. *Action Taken Report on the Part I & II of the Reports of the Fifth State Finance Commission*. Thiruvananthapuram: GoK.

Heller, Patrick, K. N. Harilal, and Shubham Chaudhari. 2007. 'Building Local Democracy: Evaluating the Impact of Decentralisation in Kerala, India'. *World Development* 35 (4): 626–648.

Kodoth, Praveena, and U. S. Mishra. 2011. 'Gender Equality in Local Governance in Kerala'. *Economic & Political Weekly* 46 (38): 36–43.

Local Self Government Department. 2013. *12th Five Year Plan (2012–17), Revised Guidelines for Plan Formulation, Subsidies and Allied matters* (Malayalam). Thiruvananthapuram: LSGD.

Mathur, Om Prakash. 2006. 'Local Government Organisation and Finance: Urban India'. In *Local Governance in Developing Countries* (pp. 169–204), edited by Anwar Shah. Washington, DC: World Bank.

Mohanakumar, S. 2002. From People's Plan to Plan sans People. *Economic & Political Weekly* 37 (16): 1492–1497.

———. 2003. Decentralisation in Kerala: People's Plan. *Economic & Political Weekly* 38 (30): 3214–3216.

Mohanakumar, S., and R Vipinkumar. 2011. 'Local Government and Market Intervention under Decentralisation: A Case Study of Vellanad Gram Panchayat, Kerala'. *Journal of Rural Development* 30 (4): 433–450.

Momoniat, Ismail. 2001. *Fiscal Decentralisation in South Africa: A Practitioner's Perspective*. Pretoria: Intergovernmental Relations Division, National Treasury.

Narayana, D. 2005. 'Local Governance without Capacity Building: Ten Years of Panchayati Raj'. *Economic & Political Weekly* 40 (26): 2822–2832.

National Institute of Rural Development. 2001. *India Panchayat Raj Report 2001: Four Decades of Decentralised Governance in Rural India (Volume I&II)*. Hyderabad: NIRD.

Oommen, M. A. (2004). 'Fiscal Decentralisation in Kerala'. In *Fiscal Decentralisation to Rural Governments in India*, edited by Geeta Sethi. New Delhi: Oxford University Press.

———. 2006. 'Fiscal Decentralisation to the Sub-State Level Governments'. *Economic & Political Weekly* 41 (10): 897–903.

———, ed. 2008. *Fiscal Decentralisation to Local Governments in India*. New Castle: Cambridge Scholars Publishing.

Oommen, M. A. 2014. 'Deepening Democracy and Local Governance: Challenges before Kerala'. *Economic & Political Weekly* 49 (25): 42–46.

Oommen, M A., Sally Wallace, and Abdu Muwonge. 2017. 'Towards Streamlining Panchayat Finance in India: A Study Based on Gram Panchayats in Kerala'. *Economic & Political Weekly* 52 (38): 49–58.

Planning Commission. 2006. *Evaluation Report on Decentralised Experience of Kerala*. Report No. 195. New Delhi: Programme Evaluation Organisation.

Prakash, B. A. 1999. *Janakeeyasoothranam, Onnam Varsha Padhathi [Manorama Year Book]* (Malayalam). Kottayam: Manorama.

———. 2005a. 'Decentralised Planning in Kerala'. In *Kerala Economy* (pp. 307–334), edited by D. Rajasenan and Gerald de Groot. Cochin: Cochin University of Science and Technology.

Prakash, B. A. 2005b. *Report of the Study on Mandatory Functions: Social Welfare Schemes and Maintenance of Assets of Local Self Government Institutions in Kerala*. Thiruvananthapuram: Department of Economics, University of Kerala (Unpublished).

Prakash, B. A., P. Krishnakumar, N. Niyathi, and R. P. Nair. 2013. *Effectiveness of Service Delivery in Panchayat Raj Institutions: Report on a Survey of Grama Panchayats in Kerala*. Thiruvananthapuram: Rajiv Gandhi Institute of Development Studies.

Prakash B A. 2018. 'Rejection of Kerala's Fifth state Finance Commission Recommendations'. *Economic and Political Weekly* 53(13): 21–24.

Raghunandan, ed. 2015. *Decentralisation and Local Governments: The Indian Experience*. New Delhi: Orient BlackSwan.

Sankaran, P. N. 2006. *Decentralisation: Institutions, Justice and Social Development in India*. New Delhi: Serials Publications.

Shah, Anwar. 2004. *Fiscal Decentralisation in Developing and Transition Economies: Progress, Problems and the Promise*. World Bank Policy Research Working Paper No. 3282. Washington, DC: World Bank.

———, ed. 2006. *Local Governance in Developing Countries*. Washington, DC: World Bank.

Shah, Anwar, and Sana Shah. 2006. 'The New Vision of Local Governance and the Evolving Roles of Local Governments'. In *Local Governance in Developing Countries* (pp. 1–46), edited by Anwar Shah. Washington, DC: World Bank.

Sharma, Rashmi. 2003. 'Kerala's Decentralisation: Idea in Practice'. *Economic & Political Weekly* 38 (36): 3832–3850.

Raghuram, Shobha. 2000. 'Kerala's Democratic Decentralisation: History in the Making'. *Economic & Political Weekly* 35 (25): 2105–2107.

Srivastava, D. K. 2008. 'Fiscal Decentralisation at the Sub-State Level in India: Some Lessons from Kerala'. In *Fiscal Decentralisation to Local Governments in India* (pp. 102–125), edited by M. A. Oommen. New Castle: Cambridge Scholars Publishing.

State Finance Commission. 1996. *State Finance Commission: Final Report*. Thiruvananthapuram: Government of Kerala.

———. 2001. *Second State Finance Commission, Kerala: Report Part I*. Thiruvananthapuram: Government of Kerala.

State Finance Commission. 2005. *Third State Finance Commission, Kerala: Report with Action Taken Report*. Thiruvananthapuram: Government of Kerala.

———. 2011. *Report of the Fourth State Finance Commission, Kerala: Part I & II*. Thiruvananthapuram: Government of Kerala.

———. 2015. *Report of the Fifth State Finance Commission: Part I*. Thiruvananthapuram: Government of Kerala.

———. 2016. *Report of the Fifth State Finance Commission: Part II*. Thiruvananthapuram: Government of Kerala.

Steffensen, Jesper, and Svend Trollegaard. 2000. *Fiscal Decentralisation and Sub-National Government Finance in Relation to Infrastructure and Service Provision*. Washington, DC: World Bank.

Thomas Isaac, T. M., and Richard Franke. 2000. *Local Democracy and Development: People's Campaign for Decentralised Planning in Kerala*. New Delhi: Left World Press.

Thomas Isaac, T. M., and K. N. Harilal. 1997. 'Planning for Empowerment: People's Campaign for Decentralised Planning in Kerala'. *Economic & Political Weekly* 32 (1–2): 53–58.

Thomas Isaac, T. M., and Patrick Heller. 2003. 'Democracy and Development: Decentralised Planning in Kerala'. In *Deepening Democracy: Institutional Innovations in Empowered Participatory Governance, the Real Utopias Project IV*, edited by Archon Fung and Erik Olin Wright. New York, NY: Verso Books.

Vijayanand, S. M. 2009. *Kerala—A Case Study of Classical Democratic Decentralisation*. Thrissur: Kerala Institute of Local Administration.

World Bank. 2004. *Fiscal Decentralisation to Rural Governments in India*. New Delhi: Oxford University Press.

———. 2009. *Local Government Discretion and Accountability: Application of a Local Governance Framework*. Report No. 49059-GLB. Washington, DC: World Bank.

ABOUT THE AUTHOR

B. A. Prakash is a former Professor and Head, Department of Economics, University of Kerala, Kariavattom, Thiruvananthapuram. Earlier, he was a professor in the Department of Economics, University of Calicut, Kerala, where he had been teaching since 1976. After retirement from the University, he was appointed as chairman of Kerala Public Expenditure Review Committee for three years by the Government of Kerala. Professor Prakash has been conducting research on different topics relating to Kerala's economic development during the last four decades and published a number of papers in leading journals, research reports and monographs. One topic in which he did research is on decentralization and local governance in Kerala. He has authored two research studies sponsored by 3rd State Finance Commission of Kerala and National Institute of Rural Development, Hyderabad. During the tenure as chairman of the 5th SFC (2015–2016), he got opportunity to conduct in-depth study on the finances of local governments and the fiscal decentralization experience of Kerala. This monograph is the outcome of his research on decentralization. Professor Prakash has edited two books on Indian economy examining the economic reforms and performance since 1991 and published in 2009 and 2012. He has also edited four books on Kerala's economic development, covering the development of the state economy since its formation and up to 2018 and published by SAGE in 1994, 1999, 2004 and 2018.

INDEX